reaching
kids
most youth
ministries
miss

Loveland, Colorado

REACHING KIDS MOST YOUTH MINISTRIES MISS

Copyright © 2000 Group Publishing, Inc.

Visit our Web site: **www.grouppublishing.com**

CREDITS
Contributing Authors: Cathi Basler, Bo Boshers, Karen Dockrey, Andy Fletcher, Marvin Jacobo, Dan Jessup, Linda Klimek, Robert Klimek, Scott J. Larson, Larry Lindquist, Julie Meiklejohn, D. Scott Miller, Mary Somerville, Patrick F. Sprankle, and Tony Tamberino
Editor: Amy Simpson
Creative Development Editor: Jim Kochenburger
Chief Creative Officer: Joani Schultz
Copy Editor: Dena Twinem
Designer and Art Director: Jean Bruns
Cover Designer: Jeff A. Storm
Computer Graphic Artist: Fred Schuth
Illustrator: Otto Pfannschmidt
Production Manager: Alexander Jorgensen

Unless otherwise noted, Scripture taken from the HOLY BIBLE, NEW INTERNATIONAL VERSION®. Copyright © 1973, 1978, 1984 by International Bible Society. Used by permission of Zondervan Publishing House. All rights reserved.

LIBRARY OF CONGRESS CATALOGING-IN-PUBLICATION DATA
Reaching kids most youth ministries miss
     p. cm.
  ISBN 0-7644-2148-4 (alk. paper)
  1. Church work with teenagers. I. Group Publishing.

BV4447 .R385 2000
259'.23--dc21   99-054693

10 9 8 7 6 5 4 3 2   09 08 07 06 05 04 03 02 01 00

Printed in the United States of America.

contents

introduction

DR. DAVE RAHN • Director • Huntington College Link
Institute...*for faithful and effective youth ministry* • Huntington, Indiana

Youth ministry that does not take seriously the charge to reach young people for Christ and establish them in his Church is a self-indulgent luxury we cannot afford.

Every time we church members call someone aside—commission them—to minister "in unique ways" to adolescents, we affirm a defining reality of youth ministry: *Teenagers are different.* Their differences set them apart from every other age group in the church. Their differences invite strategic ministry responses.

Some differences are rooted in the natural development process common to all of us. The teenage years are marked by physical changes accompanying puberty. Kids grow stronger and bigger (often at uneven paces), experience body odor, and can reproduce. During this window of development, the capacity to think in new and exciting ways, to consider hypothetical situations, and to apply imagination to real-life problem-solving emerges. Expanded levels of moral reasoning are made possible during this time. With very few exceptions, we youth workers can count on kids' genetic time-release capsules to work their wonder during the teenage years.

Other differences are rooted in the confusing expectations teenagers feel as they move into society. They wrestle with their own sense of identity, start to see themselves as different from their parents, and try to sort out their uniqueness in relation to their peers. Their need is to "individuate," to learn how to "fly" on their own. Societal benchmarks sometimes help, sometimes confound the process. At sixteen a teenager can drive, at seventeen R-rated movies are accessible, and at eighteen voting is an option and availability for military service an obligation. There is no agreed-upon, formal transition from childhood to adulthood in our society, just this fuzzy period called "adolescence."

Each of these sets of differences establishes a need in the church for the common big tent of strategic responses we have come to call "youth ministry." But as we youth workers move within the tent, we quickly realize that there are also some significant differences *among* teenagers. Sometimes these differences are rooted in the peculiar ways that teenagers huddle together while they begin their journey to blend in with the rest of us. In these cases it makes sense to target our ministry to meaningful clusters of teenagers. Other times we notice that, while teenagers might be helpfully *described* by common characteristics, they do not experience affinity groups to which they belong. They are cut off and feel very alone; our ministries need to be flavored by tutor/mentor strategies.

Differences common to teenagers as well as those separating teenagers from one another combine to make a compelling case for the strategic need for youth ministry in the church. Kids who are "out there" need to be brought into the warm, loving fellowship of Jesus Christ... "in here."

It's only when we get our hands dirty in the kind of bridge-building described in this book that we realize that, for practical purposes, the "big tent" is really a myth. There is no common locale where everyone is conveniently hanging out together until we can rescue them in Jesus' name. Instead, there are hundreds (thousands?) of special interest clumps of teenagers, millions of isolated individuals, each of whom needs to be reached out to in ways that help him or her understand the hope of a new life through Jesus Christ.

Once these widely different young people are reached for Jesus Christ, our job is not nearly complete. They still need to be forged together into a healthy group and assimilated into the body of Christ. Our Lord set high standards to measure these efforts. We know that we are different from one another; that's evidenced by the unique diversity of our gifts and experiences. But the Lord is glorified when we are unified in ways characterized by an unusual degree of love and appreciation for each other.

Each time we encounter a teenager that doesn't quite fit the youth group, our stability is threatened. Because of this disruption, some forsake the task of helping those who are outsiders join us on the inside. They believe preserving unity is more important than anything else, not realizing that they have unwittingly exchanged man-designed homogeneity for Jesus-gifted *koinonia*. When we consistently build bridges to different teenagers we become keenly aware of how dependent we are on the Lord to "build his house"; biblical unity is a gift from God. Let this book stretch your vision beyond those who currently show up in your youth group. You'll experience new tensions and frustrations. Celebrate the headaches as indicators of your increasing faithfulness.

Some of what you will read in the pages that follow should be clearly applied to the task of youth evangelism. Other insights are more helpful for the assimilation task. We want every type of Christian young person to enter into a satisfying relationship with the church. In many ways this distinction should not matter. Building bridges to persons that are different from us is a mindset that is necessary for both tasks. And both tasks are necessary if we are to be faithful to our youth ministry calling.

Is there need to review the biblical basis for labeling bridge-building as an indicator of faithfulness? Jesus' incarnation is the ultimate act of building a bridge, and Philippians 2:5-11 helps us to wonder at the love that motivated such selflessness. Paul made it clear that his own natural preferences were of no consequence in his drive to win others to Christ (1 Corinthians 9:19-23). Jesus' strategy for connecting with Zacchaeus (Luke 19:1-9) was considerably different from his strategy with the woman at the well (John 4:1-42) or Nicodemus (John 3:1-21); his bridge-building expertise is demonstrated throughout the Gospels. When we remember that God demonstrated his extravagant, aggressive love (Romans 8:35-39) for us "while we were still sinners" (Romans 5:8), it is not hard for us to agree to embrace the ministry of reconciliation that we have been assigned (2 Corinthians 5:11-21). "Reconciliation" is just a deeper, richer version of "building bridges."

Here's a tip for reading this book. As you move through each chapter, think of particular kids in your ministry, past or present. I found myself thinking of Lenny while I read the chapter about building bridges to kids with disabilities, and Smitty when reading about athletes. Brent came to mind as I read about gifted and talented teenagers, and Gloria's difficulties were vivid when I reviewed the teen moms chapter. Chad is someone I work with now who moves between anger and rage too often. For each of these cases, and others, I found the descriptions accurate and the practical tips insightful. I found myself wishing I had a resource like this twenty years ago.

I'd like to make one final observation. This book is further evidence that the field of youth ministry is growing wiser. It is an acknowledgment that while we know that teenagers *as a group* are worthy of specialized ministry focus, we also have learned that there are important differences *among* teenagers that must be reckoned with if we are going to be effective. We are growing in our appreciation of the need for increased specialization, both in what we understand and in what we practice. As rich as the following chapters are, it may be that there is a teenager or a group of teenagers in your world that don't fall under one of the following chapter headings. My prayer is that God will bother you with the burden and equip you with the creativity to build gospel bridges to those kids. Just as Jesus did for us.

I am glad to commend the following chapters to you. Perhaps you will write the next chapter we all need to read.

working with SWARTBACS

Reaching the Heart of Church Kids Who Hate Being There

DR. LARRY LINDQUIST • Chairman of Youth and Family Department • Denver Seminary • Denver, Colorado

"*As long as you live under my roof . . .*" In desperation, parents pull rank and use this ultimate condition in order to force their children to attend church. How many times have you *heard* it? How many times have you *used* it? In defense of the parents, the student who resists church probably is most in need of what it offers. In defense of the student, some church environments are mind numbing! What's a parent to do?

Here's another one. Mom and Dad sit in the office of the youth pastor, subtly accusing the ministry of neglecting their child. "She hates coming to church! Can't you do something to create a ministry that will make her *want* to be here?" The youth pastor sits there in a pile of guilt, frustration, and anger. What's a pastor to do? How can a youth ministry reach out to SWARTBACs (Students Who Are Required To Be At Church)?

As I write this chapter, my community in Littleton, Colorado, is still recovering from the 1999 tragedy at Columbine High School. So many stories have come out of that event. At the memorial service for Cassie Bernall, nearly seventy students committed their lives to Christ as a result of Cassie's clear "Yes" when asked by the one who murdered if she believed in God. Her testimony and level of commitment to Christ impacted those who had been apathetic or even resistant to the gospel. However, there's an interesting twist to her story. During a nationally televised interview with Brad and Misty, Cassie's parents, in the weeks after the tragedy, they shared how Cassie's life had changed in the year prior to her death. Although her parents had been actively involved in their church, Cassie had progressively slipped away from church and deeper into the occult and witchcraft. Concerned, her parents decided to put their foot down. They told Cassie she wouldn't be permitted to see the friends who had been pulling her more deeply into the occult, and would be allowed only to attend church youth group! Misty began to weep as she related how Cassie reacted to their new rule. "It was hard to hear someone you loved with all your heart tell you they hate you." Although Cassie was a classic SWARTBAC, the story doesn't end there. A few months before her death, Cassie participated in a youth retreat with her church. In the words of her father, Brad Bernall, "Cassie left for the retreat in a dark attitude. Her head was down and she was angry. When she returned, it was like she had been in a dark room when someone turned the light on." Cassie's life had been changed. She told her mother that she would prove the change in her life was real. She did.

The behavior of Cassie's parents fits perfectly into our discussion. When does a parent force a child to be a part of church? Should they? In the process of gaining a perspective on those questions, I used the Web to connect with youth pastors across the country. One after the other they responded with the same advice: "Parents shouldn't force their children to go to church." What happens if they do? Is Cassie the exception? What can youth leaders do when the "Cassies" show up in their groups?

● Four Axioms for Working With SWARTBACs:

> **Don't assume they know Christ.** If they're acting like hell-bound pagans, chances are they might be!
>
> **Don't assume *they* are the problem.** Your church or youth group might be as boring as the student perceives it to be.
>
> **Gather a great deal of information** before you make evaluation about the life of the student (school, home, siblings, history).
>
> **Remember the goal** is not to get them to attend your ministry, but to see them grow deeper in their relationships with Christ. That can happen one-on-one, in their home, or even (are you ready for this?) in another church!

● Use an alternative site for youth group. A coffeehouse, a restaurant, a park, even a cemetery!

● Get their friends interested in the group. Find out who they're attracted to and invite them personally.

● Let them go (prodigal son syndrome). In a contemporary context, I'm sure the father of the prodigal son would have been sitting in the office of the youth pastor pleading the case of his son. Bottom line came when the father let his son go. Although this is a tough thing for parents to hear, many youth pastors repeatedly told me that creating an environment of "entertainment" to attract SWARTBACs frustrates the students who come to deepen their walk with Christ. Parents of these students want the youth group to provide fun activities since it provides the "illusion" of involvement in church. The reality is that I cannot identify a single student who has been drawn back to Jesus by playing on the church basketball league or going roller skating.

● Talk with the SWARTBACs as a group. Hold an "I hate bein' here" forum to find out why they don't want to be there and to let them "vent" their feelings as a group.

● Train the core students in your youth ministry to establish relationships with SWARTBACs. A common reason SWARTBACs cite for hating church is the poor relationship with the youth pastor and others in the group.

● Find the area of their interest and speak to or share in that activity.

● Visit their rooms at home. You'll find out all kinds of things about them!

● Meet with their parents. Assess their attendance and level of involvement at church. What are their patterns of priority?

● In his book *Keeping Your Teen in Touch With God*, Robert Laurent cites the top ten reasons teenagers reject religion:

10. Lack of family harmony
9. Negative concept of religion
8. The struggle for emancipation from parents
7. Authoritarianism in parents
6. Negative peer influence
5. Poor relationship with youth pastor
4. Low self-esteem
3. Poor relationship with parents
2. Negative media influence (makes church look stupid)
1. Lack of opportunity for church involvement.

● Provide opportunities for involvement in the life of the church that are perceived as relevant. See *No More Us & Them* (Group Publishing), and consider the following ideas:

■ **Praise band participants/leaders**—organize the musical part of your meetings. Some students are incredibly creative in music. Allow them to share their original work if possible. "Battle of the bands" is a great vehicle to increase involvement of not only SWARTBACs, but their unchurched musician-friends as well.

■ **Drama group participants/leaders**—recruit and rehearse short dramatic vignettes. It's best to use humorous scripts. An audience that responds with laughter is a huge affirmation to the participants! Use the group in as many contexts as possible (church worship, children's worship, midweek clubs, youth meetings at other churches, and so on).

■ **Media coordinators**—create/locate videos or other media to augment the theme of your meetings. If you have a video camera, have them videotape youth events and create "live it again" videos set to music to be shown later or as promo for the next event.

■ **Sound technicians**—design and operate the sound system for meetings. Let them play some of "their" music before and after the meetings.

■ **Web site coordinators**—create a home page and maintain it. If they do this, visit the site yourself and interact with them about it. Have them make reports to the group about "hits" and messages from the site.

● Make them decide for themselves. SWARTBACs are usually located at Erikson's "identity-diffused" level. In *Teaching for Moral Growth*, Bonnidell Clouse writes, "[They] are seldom [in church] unless accompanied by the parent. They have little desire to be in a religious service and come only when they are made to do so. There are more interesting places to be and more interesting things to do." Erikson's identity-diffused level is characterized by teenagers who have never really grown personal conviction. They depend on the vicarious morals, values, or spirituality of someone else. Challenging SWARTBACs to develop personal convictions about issues is critically important. Their quest for fun and entertainment is often a technique used to circumvent the need to struggle with deeper identity issues. Don't let them!

- One youth pastor suggested that he has found success in taking SWART-BACs on camping trips, working on cars together, playing video games with them, or just hitting a restaurant with them.

- Overlook their immaturity and encourage them in areas of strength.

- Ask the parents not to force their students to come to church. Let the youth ministry speak for itself. That's a risky approach, but if they're freed to choose, then it's their choice. One youth pastor told me that her experience was that not only did the SWARTBACs come, but they brought friends as well!

- If parents are determined to force their children to attend church, agree on some sort of limited (consecutive) time period. After that period, arrange for the students to meet with the youth pastor to evaluate the youth ministry and share how they would make improvements.

- Develop adult prayer team relationships with specific SWARTBACs in your group. One of the greatest deficits in the life of most adolescents is strong relationships with adults. Many times SWARTBACs are rebelling against the church because of parents. Developing relationships with other adults gives them a balance and shows them maturing believers. Adults often will gently pursue them differently than their peers.

- Take them on retreats. Extended time away from home and distractions allows deeper relationships to grow with leaders and other group members. One pastor's advice to parents of SWARTBACs was, "You get them on the bus, even if they're kicking and screaming, and I'll guarantee they'll be glad they came."

- Find students in the group who will "go after" SWARTBACs. Often these students feel unwanted or unable to break into the existing group.

ideas

- Break into their lives as a teacher. For example, if you teach them how to water-ski, work on a classic Mustang, or fly, you become a teacher to them. This allows you entrance into their lives to teach other things, too!

- Look at the long term. Some students need just a strong initial push and they'll become involved. However, some students need to be convinced that they aren't simply "projects" to be forgotten once we've "bagged 'em." More than most students, SWARTBACs have built-in "superficiality detectors"! If you're going to establish a relationship with them, realize it might be long term.

- In *How to Work With Rude, Obnoxious and Apathetic Kids*, Les Christie offers six reasons why students become apathetic about church:

  - **Because churches are out of touch.** Know what the students are talking about. What do *they* read? What do *they* watch? Take a little survey sometime and be amazed at how much you don't know about their world.

  - **Because they have no friends in church.** This can be either perceived or reality. If students don't believe anyone at church cares for them, is it any wonder they resist attending? As best you can, challenge some of the other students to link themselves with SWARTBACs.

  - **Because of senioritis (impending graduation).** To address this problem, some churches are holding their confirmation/membership classes in the fall of the senior year to avoid overlapping with high school graduation. This way it's more difficult for the seniors to equate separation from school with separation from church. It also provides an entire year to strengthen the link with the church.

  - **Because church is boring.** Encourage the students to find creative (doesn't always have to be expensive) ways to jazz up the group time. One of the main concerns should be pace. That will cost nothing! Keep it moving and keep it smooth! Have a "plan B" on deck as often as possible to throw into the mix just to catch up any "dead air" that happens. Be as unpredictable as you can. Howard Hendricks challenged me long ago that high predictability produces low impact. Low predictability produces high impact.

  - **Because they fear failure.** Create a safe environment for all students. Admit your own failures. As often as possible, eliminate competition in your youth group. As attractive as winning is, for every winner there is an equal or greater number of losers. Teenagers live in a highly competitive world. Work to reduce that stress. Set up programs that don't encourage domination by superstars. Create games that are so unique that no one person can dominate (strobe light volleyball, earthball soccer).

■ **Because they need spiritual regeneration.** As I stated in the axioms of reaching SWARTBACs, don't assume that simply because they've hung out at church all their lives, they've committed their lives to Christ. If they haven't, don't expect that they'll desire to be with those who have. One of the unfortunate oversights on the part of many youth pastors is simply asking students for their personal faith stories! How many of your current students have shared theirs with you? SWARTBACs are the toughest, since they know all the jargon to use.

● Move from an adult-led to a student-led ministry. Ministry that is done *to* students rather than *with* students is bound to push them away.

● Hold an "I have a dream" night. Everyone is asked to share what he or she would like to be doing in twenty years. Some won't have a clue, so you might want to have some categories to stimulate some discussion. Inspire them to greatness.

● Take Les Christie's advice: "In youth work we have mistakenly assumed that the best way to relate to young people is to provide them with various forms of entertainment. Maybe instead we should invite young people to accept the challenge to become heroes and change the world" *(How to Work With Rude, Obnoxious and Apathetic Kids)*.

● Make sure everything you share has applicability. A good rule is that at least 50 percent should be content, and the rest should be application (narratives, stories, and illustrations).

● Take the students to cross-cultural events. They don't have to be long-distance events. One junior high group spent a week studying the whole issue of sex, AIDS, and prostitution. The following week, the leaders surprised the students by packing up the church bus and driving down to 7th Street, where prostitution took place. The students got off the bus and stood in a local parking lot while a police officer (a member of the church in full uniform) spoke to the students about his experiences with that world. The students were highly motivated to listen and learn. The next week, even the SWARTBACs were bringing friends!

● Don't get caught in the myth that it's your *highest* obligation to attend to the SWARTBACs. Jesus didn't spend all his time and energy trying to establish relationships with the Pharisees in hope that they would develop a hunger for God. Rather, he invested in twelve men who wanted to be with him. You should attend to the SWARTBACs in your group, but never to the extent that you neglect those who are seeking to follow Christ.

● Begin to develop a decentralized youth ministry. In the September/October 1998 issue of Youthworker, Jeff Greer outlines a youth ministry philosophy that programs various events to attract a diversity of target groups. Rather than creating a single event and hoping all the students will show up, we need to create various off-campus events that will attract a target group of students. For those who would ask how we would gather all the target groups together, Greer answers with the question "Why do we have to bring them all together?"

● Ultimately, it's the parents' responsibility. As ministers to youth, we need to create an environment where students feel accepted, safe, welcomed, and genuinely loved. However, the bottom line is that parents have to get the kids there. We can't bypass the parents in youth ministry, and they can't put the complete blame on us for their children's noninvolvement. Youth and family ministry means a team effort.

outside the church walls

Ministering to Unchurched Teenagers

CHAPTER

2

LINDA KLIMEK • Religious Educator • Our Lady of Fatima Church • Lakewood, Colorado

The information age has created a world of disconnection. On TV the story about a person winning a golf tournament is packaged in the same thirty-second slot as the report of a thousand deaths in a war. In the same afternoon, without training or preparation, video arcades allow a player to shoot it out in the wild west and to go hang gliding over the Grand Canyon. Teenagers deal with disjointedness by connecting to some type of specialized peer group (such as Jocks or Goths), a group that may exclude them from participating in another.

Forty years ago, Sunday services were a common part of family experience. Regardless of the teenager's disposition, absence was not an option. During this period of time, the pace of life moved according to a family rhythm. Things developed and changed in months and years, not in seconds. Today it's typical for a sixty-second television commercial to show a person bathing in the morning, running off to work, meeting with a friend for lunch, and taking in the opera at night—all on the same brand of deodorant soap. This quick no-nonsense world is designed to attract interest and instant participation (spending). Unfortunately, this lifestyle has no relationship to the actual rhythm of life.

Church services are paced more like a traditional Thanksgiving dinner: slow and deliberate, filled with mistakes, laughter, cleanups, and lots of conversation. Churched teenagers are willing to slow down and take in this world. Unlike their peers of forty years ago, however, this places them in a class by themselves. Called "WWJDs" and "Churchies" by their peers, their dress and manner are viewed by unchurched teenagers as yet another subculture. Consequently, if unchurched youth wish to join a church family, they must be willing to face the dual challenge of understanding the counterculture pace of church and joining a group that may be unacceptable to their current set of friends.

Churches can inadvertently reinforce alienation by telegraphing messages of disinterest to their youth. These hidden agendas unintentionally aid in the first step of isolation the unchurched youth undergoes. Consider what is being said when all youth services and activities are held outside regular adult service times. What do teenagers perceive when parents of fidgety children are constantly encouraged to step outside? Unwittingly, these and other actions may be interpreted as an "unwelcome mat" to all but the established of the congregation. Teenagers sense hypocrisy at work here and easily use this as an excuse to move away from the church family.

Everyone needs to excel at something, especially teenagers. These pre-adults long to contribute to and be appreciated by a group. "Inexperienced" Christian youth find it difficult to be a part of a church group where they must assume the role of amateur, or even klutz. Initially, these fringe teenagers feel that they lack the necessary social graces and know-how to practice religion in a formal setting. This isn't attractive to a teenager who needs to stand out and excel.

For teenagers at this unchurched level, the whole concept of practicing faith is lost. While youth are familiar with sports figures, movie stars, and contemporary musicians practicing a particular art form or discipline, the teenagers can't relate this routine to the weekly discipline of church. In comparison to the world where they practice, the constantly entertaining electronic realm, Sunday services appear archaic, stilted, and meaningless. Unfortunately, this situation may tempt the unchurched to view themselves as unworthy and unqualified to be Christians.

Consider this story:

> At age ninety-nine, Antonio was told to get new friends. At this time in his life, he found he couldn't count on his old ones. Immediately, Antonio had an idea. Going into town, he sought out Soli, a carpenter, and hired him to construct a plain pine door. Two weeks later, Antonio picked up the finished door and took it to the town square. There he leaned it against the trunk of an ancient oak tree. After soundly stating, "Now, I am ready to make new friends!" Antonio quietly returned to his home.
>
> Curious villagers began to wander up to the door. Slowly it became a town custom to gather around it every evening and discuss its presence. Picnickers would set their blankets near it. Children played hide and seek behind it. The door became the centerpiece of the annual spring carnival. Sidewalk sales and church event fliers were tacked on it. By the end of one year it was common to hear people say things like "Wait for me by the door" and "Go down to the door and take a right."
>
> At the end of an entire year, at age 100, Antonio retrieved the door. Taking it home, he hung the door in his front doorway, sat down on a chair, and began rocking.
>
> Immediately the town lost its bearings. Questions like "Where should we meet?" and "How do I get there?" needed new answers. Word got around that the door was at Antonio's house. Everyone gradually drifted to his porch. As each new person approached, the calm Antonio greeted him or her by saying, "Welcome, you already know my front door, so have a seat." From that day on Antonio's home became the town meeting place, and Antonio was forever blessed with friends—young and old.

While we may not need to carry a "welcome door" to shopping centers and video arcades, we may need just such a dramatic and tangible idea to attract the youth to our doorways. Like Antonio, we will need to familiarize them with our doorway, even before they consider the possibility of joining the church youth group.

So how do we effectively create a "welcome door" for youth ministry?

● Remind your church of the welcoming message of Jesus toward the woman at the well (John 4:4-42). Jesus allowed the woman some space and a stress-free environment in which to experience his presence. It's important for us to do the same for the unchurched.

- Teenagers often feel the church is unaware of what's really going on in the world. They easily believe church leadership to be ignorant of the multiple pressures in their lives. In view of this, consider creating a youth "listening post." Before stethoscopes, doctors used small wooden posts to listen to the chest cavities of patients. This was a way of monitoring the heart. In a similar manner, gather around a candle regularly and listen to the hearts of the youth.

- Put out fliers in your geographic area announcing the current issues to be discussed at your "listening post."

- Bring in experts (such as police, juvenile officers, radio personalities, and religious leaders) not only to inform, but also to listen.

- If the crowd is small, change the meeting location. Be willing to be a traveling youth group.

- Count up your church events. Notice what proportion is given to the elderly, the youth, the children, parents with children, and so on. Is there time parity between them?

- Reach out to parents with children. While children are between the ages of one and eight, many anxious parents are embarrassed by the behavior of their children. This can lead them to stay away until the children get older. This is a model a child can pick up and continue to follow.

- If possible, even for a small portion of the Sunday service, keep the children in church. Keep families together. Occasionally forgo the sermon. Spend time compassionately helping unacquainted churchgoers with the rhythm and pace of prayer.

- Regularly remind the church community that they need to show love toward children and what they consequently become, youth.

- Adopt the feeling of Ephesians 4:25. The unchurched affect us directly and at all times. Consider what it would be like if the entire world showed up for church this Sunday and wanted to actively and enthusiastically participate. How would that compare to a typical, middle-of-February church service? Now is it easier to sense the "incompleteness" in all our congregations on any given Sunday? Is it important that the worshipping assembly feel and be activated by this?

- Don't publicly use the term "unchurched" or any other labels that divide people. A father with two daughters got into the habit of calling one brilliant and the other dumb. After years of this conditioning, the first daughter became the head of surgery for a prestigious research hospital. The other daughter satisfied her father's prediction and slipped into prostitution. Words can and do alienate.

- Once unchurched teenagers have found a home with your group, build up common "family" experiences with them. Develop unforgettable events that will build attachments to the church family.

- Nothing should be considered too silly or purposeless. Even an unplanned (outdoor) gelatin fight can forge new group relationships.

- Increase the visibility of the youth in your church. Welcome teenagers in your ministry of greeting. Let them fill a variety of fun roles that will help them discover their particular gifts. Remember, if you want the job done, make it a fun task.

- Have a discussion about fun. Is church fun? What does that mean? How is fun different from entertainment? Did Jesus ever have fun in his ministry? One definition of fun is "something that provides enjoyment." Where is the enjoyment in church?

- Befriend experts in teenagers' fields of interest. This could include skateboarders, dance and volleyball instructors, coaches, and others. Hold an "Ultimate Learning" day when teenagers from the local community can be present to learn tips from the pros.

- Don't try to sign up everyone for something immediately. Let your youth group regulars act as models and quiet hosts. Let the unchurched teenagers get used to the pace and rhythm of being around churched people.

- At one time, the church home was a stress-free environment. Today, for a variety of reasons, it may not be. Many teenagers feel a great deal of disruption and confusion in their lives. They won't feel attracted to a church that is weathering internal storms. Minimize conflict and deal with it in healthy ways when it arises.

- When asked, be honest and frank about your denomination. Never gloss over the details. Let the questioning teenager know that life in a family can have good and bad times.

- If teenagers truly feel loved by their church family, quitting won't be an option during rough times.

- Remember: Don't just maintain a youth organization, get your church to love it into reaching its fullest potential.

- Alert the church to their role as "prospectors." Remind them that they must look for and find every precious gem that comes into their presence.

- Alert parents that a "keeping the kid busy" mentality may be burdening their teenagers with an overwhelming amount of other practice (for soccer, baseball, and gymnastics) without any church "practice."

- Challenge your youth group to do a daily mirror prayer. How? On a daily basis (such as in the morning, before school), each young person should spend a moment looking into a mirror. Have them stay there until they see the "face of God" looking back at them. Then as they move into the community, it should be easier to see the face of God in others, especially the unchurched.

- Consider the story of Zacchaeus (Luke 19:1-10). He was almost "unchurched" because of his size. The disabled, minority families, and others may feel alienated by circumstances and not by choice. Keep an eye out for them!

- From time to time, all youth leaders wake up feeling like Antonio—ninety-nine years old and friendless. Don't let this natural feeling paralyze your effort to find the unchurched. Go out, create a "welcome door," and begin making new friends for the future of your church family.

healing life's hurts

Ministering to Abused Youth

PATRICK F. SPRANKLE · Coordinator of Youth
Ministry · St. Louis Catholic Church · Clarksville, Maryland

hen Sara entered my office after school with a friend, I knew something was wrong. The stark change in her normally outgoing personality, the uncontrollable sobbing, and the way she gently cupped her face in her hands all indicated a crisis moment. Sara soon confided in me that her father had hit her in the face in a drunken rage (a bruise in the shape of his hand left a clear mark of his violence). Sara not only was in physical pain but also spoke of the agony, disappointment, and distrust she felt because someone she loved had hurt her so aggressively. Sara needed immediate intervention and assurance that she would be protected in the future.

Sara had some positive healing moments during this traumatic time. Friends and family provided listening ears and shoulders to cry on. Agency representatives were compassionate advocates for her situation. Sara's church community stood solidly with her through it all.

Sara's story is all too familiar in youth ministry and in a world where chaos, violence, and unsafe homes and schools are becoming more prevalent. According to Prevent Child Abuse America, 1997 saw over 3 million *reported* incidences of child abuse and neglect in the United States. Sara's situation wasn't typical, though. Many young people who are exposed to long-term abusive relationships aren't able to find (or trust) the resources necessary to help them through their ordeals.

Young people face a variety of struggles as they cope with the heavy burden of abuse. Families deal with complex issues like substance abuse, divorce, and poor conflict-management and communication skills. Many young people also know that further conflict might occur if protective agencies become involved and many will continue to protect those who are responsible for inflicting the pain. Finally, those young survivors of abuse and neglect are often told to "keep it in the family" because of shame or an unhealthy sense of pride.

Youth workers who suspect abuse often run into a wall of silence when attempting to minister to the needs of these hurting youth. Abuse is naturally a very sensitive topic. Parents, school officials, and church leaders are sometimes hesitant to address the issue in religious or academic instruction or from the pulpit.

Young people themselves are understandably tentative about sharing the "secrets" of an unhealthy relationship, and often need professional counseling to begin telling their stories.

However difficult, youth workers have the responsibility and the privilege to reach out and minister to the needs of abused youth. As disciples of Jesus, youth workers can act as his instruments of healing and peace. "Come to me, all you who are weary and burdened, and I will give you rest" (Matthew 11:28).

Young people can be strengthened and supported by remembering Jesus' own abuse at the hands of strangers, and can be guided to turn to him in their own suffering. Youth workers who are proactive through awareness, attitude, and action can lighten many burdens and provide comfort and rest.

AWARENESS

● Be aware of the dynamics of family life in your church. Survey young people and whole families with these questions: What are the needs of parents and families? How is our church meeting these needs? How might various church ministries encourage a healthy family life?

● Familiarize yourself with agencies, institutions, and individuals that provide crisis prevention/management and counseling services. Make a list of youth-friendly people and groups who reach out to youth at risk and have it ready for immediate use. Know your limits and when to refer.

● Know what to look for. Educate yourself on the warning signs of physical, emotional, and sexual abuse. Be aware of the symptoms of neglect and mal-treatment. Indicators of abuse may include depression, poor self-image, truancy and/or change in grades, running away, chemical abuse, suicide attempts, recurrent physical complaints, overly seductive behavior, and extreme attention-getting. For a comprehensive definition of abuses and a further list of indicators, consult Safe Child (www.safechild.org).

● Visit families on their own turf and get to know them. Observe family dynamics and affirm healthy conflict-resolution styles. When a crisis arises, a positive relationship history will go a long way.

● Make sure your typical youth gathering is a safe and healthy place to hang out. Do you offer peaceful resolutions to conflicts?

ATTITUDE

● Practice the ministry of "just being there." A caring, easygoing, and listening attitude opens youth workers to all kinds of revelations! If young people feel they can just relax and feel comfortable in your presence, they'll find it easier to share critical moments with you.

● Take time to pray and read the Bible. Quiet time with God's Word can clear your mind and provide perspective when crises arise. Begin each day praying for (and with) young people in crisis.

● Make it a point to have an open-door policy. Encourage young people to stop by and have a soda as a check-in for their day. Be accessible for them after school or whenever they're free (within reason, of course!). Make house calls, school calls, mall calls, or sports calls to be visible in their lives.

● Be a peacemaker and a peace-liver. Show in your own attitudes the power of God's peace and the strength of inner calm. Work to be an example in your own relationships.

● Let young people know in words and actions that you're open to hearing anything they're going through. Accept and affirm feelings. Caringly and carefully challenge inappropriate displays of anger. Practice not being too shocked or embarrassed or angry or disappointed when someone talks about abuse.

ACTION

● Be able to intervene when necessary. Young people who disclose an abusive relationship need prompt attention and instant action. Your knowledge and immediate response will allow a young person to see that someone is taking control of a very chaotic time in their lives.

● Organize a support group for survivors of child abuse, date rape, incest, or any other violent act. Consult a therapist specializing in the field, or even invite a local professional to facilitate the group.

● Train adults and young people to be "abuse responders." Conduct seminars to teach abuse indicators and listening skills. Use peer ministry training like the format in *Teen to Teen: Responding to Peers in Crisis* (St. Mary's Press) or *Training Youth for Dynamic Leadership* (Group Publishing).

● Hold a town meeting on abuse. Invite the press, pastors, and parents. Discuss the issues and a Christian response. Coordinate professionals from health services and survivors of abuse to raise awareness of and action for people in abusive relationships.

● Support legislation that protects the rights and dignity of those who are abused. Be a voice in church and community for those who sometimes have no voice.

● Help local shelters and residential treatment centers for abused people. Coordinate fund-raisers to provide material assistance. Volunteer time and talent to support the day-to-day operations of the shelters.

● Make your youth ministry family-based. Provide day or weekend retreats where young people and their parents can reflect together about family roles, traditions, communication, and dealing with differences. Encourage positive outlets to family dynamics by offering parent/teen sports, intergenerational games and other events, churchwide plays or talent shows, and family appreciation dinners.

● Offer a three- to four-week speaker series on healthy relationships. Cover such themes as "sexual con games" (*Unmasking Sexual Con Games*, 2nd Edition, Ron W. Herron and Kathleen M. Sorenson, M.A. 1997), managing conflicts, effective communication skills, surviving abusive relationships, one hundred ways to show affection, dealing with stress and unrealistic expectations, and being a friend to someone in crisis.

- Create a Web page giving information on where to go for help when dealing with a crisis, especially if being abused. Attractive posters announcing the Web address can be placed in the church bulletin, local schools, malls, fast-food restaurants, and other places where young people hang out.

- Encourage young people to perform a "ministry of child care," freely helping young parents and other families who may be experiencing stressful home situations. Provide special baby-sitting services during peak holiday seasons for those parents who need to go shopping.

- Organize a twenty-four-hour crisis hot line with other churches in your area. Offer crisis counseling, referral services, and prevention ideas.

- Form partnerships with area middle and high schools, offering crisis help to overburdened administrators. While confidentiality is essential, youth workers can be objective sounding boards if young people are having difficulty due to abusive relationships.

- Use images from the media to discuss creative and peaceful solutions to conflicts. Popular movie clips, songs, commercials, and the Internet can be catalysts to reflections on Christian values like peacemaking and nonviolent behaviors.

- Conduct five- to ten-minute "how to" sessions at the end of meetings, lock-ins, leadership board gatherings, or church services. Teach practical skills like how to say "no" when pressured to have sex, how to survive when a person becomes violent or inappropriately angry, how to prevent date rape, how to share thoughts and feelings in a conflict situations, and more.

- Create a plan for "safe homes" with church and community groups or individuals. If a young person needs to make a sudden move out of a home, be ready with people who are committed and competent in providing shelter or any other assistance.

- Coordinate a Bible study on a topic related to abuse: "Peace that the world cannot give" (John 14:27), "People we love who hurt us" (Psalm 55:12-14), Jesus' mission statement: "The Spirit of the Lord is on me" (Luke 4:16-18), or Jesus' death and resurrection.

- Conduct a church poster or essay contest and have participants submit reflections on the one of the following statements:

    Abuse (or violence) is…

God's healing power sometimes looks like…
To be a temple of the Holy Spirit means…
An illustration (or essay) of Matthew 11:28 might be…

● Publicize "24 Ways You Can Prevent Child Abuse" (www.kidspeace.org) and use it as a discussion starter for your next meeting with parents. Ask parents for their success stories.

● Make a "peace pledge" available to families, dating couples, schools, and community organizations. Have individuals sign the pledges, committing themselves to…

Live in peace and act in hope.
Pray for those affected by violence or abuse.
Seek out a wise and trusted adult if abused or know someone who is abused.

● Pray for your young people, especially those who are abused or neglected. The greatest impetus to change comes through the power of prayer!

giving oil to the wheel that doesn't squeak
Reaching Shy Students

MARVIN JACOBO · Minister to High School Students (with wife Cheryl and daughter Dayna) · First Baptist Church · Modesto, California

Shy people withdraw, pull back, draw in, shrink, cringe, flinch, and blush. They feel bashful, self-conscious, reserved, inarticulate, backward, embarrassed, fearful, apprehensive, suspicious, and cowardly. These students in your ministry won't be squeaking for oil like others do. But without being generously oiled, they'll disappear as silently as they came.

Working with shy students, the youth worker's first challenge is to determine if the student is shy (afraid of people) or just quiet (an introvert that doesn't gain emotional energy from being with people). Students and leaders need to know the difference. Even extroverts can be shy and timid.

What causes shyness? It could come from the student's natural temperament or a family background of having shy parents. Feelings of inadequacy could come from domination by parents, siblings, or others. Perhaps the person has experienced failure or has been ridiculed. Whatever the seed that was planted in his or her life, it sprouted into a root of fear.

BIBLICAL EXAMPLE

One biblical example of ministering to a timid soul is Paul's ministry to Timothy. Paul had kindled a fire in this young man by giving him blessings. Then as Paul noticed that Timothy's shyness was keeping him from using his spiritual gifts and abilities, Paul had to rekindle that fire and spur him on to good works. Read 2 Timothy 1, and notice Paul's methods of bringing Timothy out of his fear of people into a fulfillment of who God made him to be. Here's how to relate Paul's example to encouraging your shy students:

● **Verse 3**—Express gratefulness to them for their presence in the group, acknowledging that they make a difference. Tell them you're praying for them!

● **Verse 4**—It's easy not to notice these kids in a crowd, but how special they feel when you go out of your way with enthusiasm to greet them. Let them know you look forward to seeing them again.

● **Verse 5**—Assume the very best of them and express what you know to be true about them.

● **Verse 6**—To challenge these students toward strength and boldness, do what Paul did—place your hands on them and give them a blessing. These are the five elements of a biblical blessing as found in *The Gift of the Blessing* by Gary Smalley and John Trent, Ph.D.:

   meaningful touch,

   spoken words of affirmation,

   attaching high value to the one being blessed,

   picturing a special future for the one being blessed, and

   an active commitment to fulfill the blessing.

● **Verse 7**—Envision for them what God desires for them. Tell them that God has them in process to not "be afraid of people, but to be wise and strong, and to love them and enjoy being with them" (2 Timothy 1:7, The Living Bible)

● **Verses 8-12**—Ask these students to join with you in taking the risk of living by God's power. Help them feel like they'll be partners with you in your personal journeys of faith and in ministry.

● **Verses 13-14**—Challenge them to hold onto the truth about themselves and appreciate their God-given abilities and gifts. First you must teach them to understand how God wired them uniquely and how God intends to utilize them uniquely. Acceptance of themselves diminishes their fear of others.

WHAT STUDENTS SAID

As we talked with other youth workers in gathering information for this chapter, someone suggested we announce to our youth group that we were going to have a meeting for all the shy kids to come and share their ideas on the topic. This idea did not come from a shy person! It's the last thing a shy student would come to. Shy people require one-on-one relationships to increase their trust level. Then their sense of belonging and acceptance in a group can follow. Instead of a big group meeting, we gave the assignment to a willing shy student to interview other shy students one-on-one. Here are the questions asked and their responses:

How can your youth group help you feel like you're a part of the group?

- "By giving me time and attention. People make me feel I'm important by spending time with me."

- "By accepting me for who I am. I will know this when people appreciate what I'm good at; when people trust me and open up to me; when I know that no one is trying to change me because I tend to be quiet."

- "Immediate friendliness. Having people notice that I am new and taking the initiative to come up and talk to me."

- "Having people take care of me. Not just saying 'hi,' introducing themselves, and then walking away. Give me something to do and somewhere to go because the minute I start to feel helpless I get uncomfortable. Get me into a small group or have me fill out a visitor's card—something!"

- "When people talk to me, give me information. If it's my first time, I'll want to know what usually goes on. And don't talk like you're reading a manual—what's your opinion? That's bound to get my attention."

- "Please don't ignore me! Having people pay attention to me (noticing when I'm in a room or a group) is wonderful and can mean the world in getting me to come out of myself or come back."

- "Having only super-outgoing people reach out to us isn't what we want. If the people who are friendly to everyone are the only ones greeting us, it can make us feel uncomfortable. Many of us tend to have insecure and negative thoughts about others' motives. Having other quiet people come up to us as well is great because we can relate to them. Sometimes overly friendly people can scare us."

- "Having someone call me and say, 'When you get here, let's find each other and sit together.'"

- "Walking into a group alone can be terrifying. Getting a ride with friends and knowing who you're walking in with is big!"

- "When other students see me at church and then talk to me at school and ask if I'm going to other youth events."

How can your youth group help you develop friendships in the group?

- "Being in small groups doing activities and having fun, not just sitting down, so it isn't as nervous and uncomfortable."

- "Sleepovers!"

- "Having a few kids invite me along to do stuff besides church."

- "Having the leaders ask me to help them do something for other students."

- "If I continue to be shy even when people are persistent at trying to get to know me—don't give up. I will eventually come around and it might just be taking me awhile to warm up to you. Usually inside I'm dying to be friends, but my shyness holds me back."

How can your youth group help you find your place to serve?

- "Have the leaders ask me to be praying for something. This encourages me to want to get involved and help."

- "Being given more responsibility and opportunities to find out what I'm good at."

- "Having others encourage me by telling me what I would be good at."

- "Ask me to be a part of a team. Start with little stuff and then get bigger."

- "Having my leader dream big dreams for me and expanding my perspective."

- "Taking the S.H.A.P.E. profile and learning that God made me just the way he wanted me. Learning that everyone is different but important in their own way."

    In *Purpose Driven™ Youth Ministry*, author Doug Fields gives the S.H.A.P.E. tool to help people pinpoint these areas of giftedness:

    Spiritual Gifts: "How has God gifted you?"

    Heart: "What do you love to do? What are you passionate about?"

    Abilities: "What natural abilities or talents were you born with or did you develop before your relationship with Christ?"

    Personality: "How will your unique personality impact your ministry?"

    Experiences: "How can your experiences, both good and bad, be used to help others?"

- "Give everyone a spiritual gift test and teach about it so everyone appreciates each other's abilities and gifts." (One such test is from the book *The Word on Finding and Using Your Spiritual Gifts* by Jim Burns.)

What are some things a youth group should not do to a shy student?

- "Never comment on my quietness. I know I'm quiet, and it's discouraging to have someone point it out. It's definitely not a good conversation starter. (It's like pointing out a zit. I already know it's there, and I'm very self-conscious of it.)"

- "Don't put us on the spot. Don't single us out in a big group."

- "Don't ask me to do something I don't feel I can do."

- "I get very embarrassed when I'm expected to do stuff or say something in front of a big group."

- "Don't say, 'Oh wow, you talk!' Don't tell me what I need to change. I'm frustrated about how hard it is, and I've already been trying."

WHAT YOUTH WORKERS SAID

Following are ideas from some "quiet," formerly shy adult youth workers:

- Introverts make great prayer warriors. Pair up these students as prayer partners for each other and the ministry, and then watch them blossom.

- Give them a job that won't bring attention to themselves but gives them a chance to serve: sound or other technical work, computer work, creating fliers, setting up early for meetings, passing out notes, and so on.

- Personally invite them to be part of a team or committee where an objective will be worked on together. Point out to them what their personal contributions would bring to the team. In other words, make them feel needed.

- Challenge them to think differently about the "big group." To walk in thinking, "Who is by himself that I can sit with?" or "What one person can I pray for during this time?" The objective is to change their preoccupation with themselves into a preoccupation with others.

- Ask parents which other students in the group their child knows or would like to know. Ask those students to make a point to reach out and include the timid one, even calling and personally inviting him or her.

- Determine to have varied personalities within your adult ministry team. Give your students a healthy model of how different personalities and spiritual gifts can be used. Evaluate your present leadership. Is your ministry only honoring the up-front leadership gifts? Or is there a strong belief that introverts as well as extroverts can reach your youth?

● Help these students accept themselves by understanding themselves. Along with teaching on spiritual gifts, help students discover these aspects of who they are:

> **Leadership Style**—Everyone has leadership potential and ability. Shy students are free to exercise their God-given leadership once they comprehend they have it. It's important for them to understand that there are different styles and ways to be a leader. (One resource is "Finding Your Leadership Style: Ten Different Ways to Lead God's People" by Bill Hybels, Winter 1998 edition of Leadership.)

> **Personality**—It's always freeing to discover what God already knows about us. Students who understand how God has custom-designed their personalities can be accepting of others as well as themselves. (One resource is "The Keirsey Temperament Sorter" from the book *Please Understand Me* by David Keirsey and Marilyn Bates.)

> **Love Languages**—We all have emotional tanks that need to be filled, but we receive and give love differently. How students express love to others is a clue to the ways they need to receive love (Gary Chapman, *The Five Love Languages*).

seeing through God's eyes

Working With Young People Who Have Alcohol and Drug Issues

CATHI BASLER • Co-Director • Souled Out Youth Church • Mount Prospect, Illinois

As a youth worker, if you want to reach young people who have never heard the gospel message, and if you know anything about this generation, then you know about the staggering number of teenagers that are experimenting with drugs and alcohol. You know that today's kids aren't just experimenting with the casual use of "pot" and a beer or two at a party, but they're also experimenting with all forms of harder drugs.

Drugs like heroin and cocaine used to be high-ticket items, found on the streets of the inner city or in the boardrooms of white-collar workers. They weren't typically accessible to high school young people in the schools of middle America. Yet over the last few years, the doors of our local high schools have opened to hard drugs, and young people are developing addictions to cocaine and heroin and other drugs at alarming rates.

Years ago, the "just say no to drugs" campaign won an audience and for a moment it seemed the tide had turned. But with the sophistication of the drug market, its low prices, its cheap imitations, and the targeting of today's more affluent youth, there has now developed a whole generation of teenagers who no longer "just say no" and find themselves experimenting with all types of drugs and calling it "socially acceptable."

Although hard drugs have become more accessible and acceptable, not every young person uses hard drugs, and there still are many teenagers who don't approve of any form of drug use. Yet many young people do approve of underage drinking parties with occasional pot smoking and sniffing inhalants as forms of an easy high. The belief of many in this generation of young people is that in order to have fun, you must take some form of artificial stimulant.

In this chapter, I won't attempt to quote the statistics of drug and alcohol abuse. As youth workers, these statistics are in front of us every day in the forms of the faces of the young people we minister to. Rather, I'll attempt to give you some suggestions, based on what we've learned from dealing with hundreds of unchurched drug- and alcohol-addicted young people. We've seen hundreds won to the Lord, lives changed, and addictions broken. But we've also seen some die before us, and others sent to jails and hospitals for their abuse. We know that the stakes are high and it will take nothing short of a concentrated all-out effort by the church to win this young generation with the love of God.

So how do we make sure we have a youth group where God is real enough that taking drugs becomes "uncool"? A youth group whose God is big enough and is present enough that he sets free those who are in the chains of addiction? A youth group that isn't afraid to bring in young people who find themselves in these chains so they can find the love of God in the other kids and also find adults who care for them?

IT'S A BOREDOM PROBLEM

Be real, and give young people something to do. In order to fight the seduction of drugs and alcohol and peer pressure, as a leader you must have life in you! One of the main reasons these kids struggle with drugs, alcohol, and parties is the fact that they're just bored. When kids find themselves with something to do, they're less inclined to be involved in drug use.

- Balance your "fun" activities with activities that can make a difference. If you just do "fun" things (like pizza parties and bowling), you won't retain young people who struggle with these issues. You might be successful keeping your kids out of drugs, but you won't attract the local teen drug users and give them an alternative. Give all your young people a strong challenge. This not only keeps them off drugs and alcohol, it also gives their lives purpose.

- Don't be afraid to teach the true gospel message, one of sacrifice and commitment. Don't water it down. These kids won't be attracted to weak Christianity. They take big risks, why not teach them to take risks with God?

- Make your meetings exciting! Inspire and challenge young people. It's important to teach young people that God isn't just a big daddy saying, "No, don't touch that, don't do that," but he is *life*, more exciting and more real than anything else.

- Use worship at your meetings. We have an all-youth worship band, and many troubled young people find themselves worshipping with all their hearts at the meetings. There is great power in the presence of God and the consistent love and prayers of God's people.

- Develop outreach projects to people with fewer economic advantages. This is an effective way to touch the hearts of young people. We regularly take our young people to the inner city of Chicago to feed the poor and paint houses. We take some of our roughest kids and pull them out of their comfort zones. They love the challenge.

- Take your youth group to visit young people in jail. Juvenile jails are breeding grounds for hardened criminals unless they can see others who really care for them. This will not only open doors of outreach, but will be a strong wake-up call for some of the kids you might be trying to reach.

- Take kids on the mission field. Kids with drug and alcohol problems may not be the best missionaries, but mission trips can help keep kids out of trouble, open up new worlds to them, and help them see beyond themselves. They also provide goals for kids to keep their lives in line. These young people usually respond to the challenge and become your most adventurous students.

IT'S AN ADDICTION PROBLEM

Many young people's addictions actually stem from being in families where there are addiction problems. Others have chosen the lifestyle on their own. Addiction takes a lot of time to resolve and a lot of patience, but if young people truly want help, they can change. We've seen young people change quickly and quit their drug and alcohol use when they turned to Christ, but frankly, most young people need more time.

● Don't expect overnight change. Stick with kids for the long haul.

● Work with local drug abuse agencies to provide help for the teenagers you work with.

● Begin a Narcotics and Alcoholics Anonymous group for young people. We open our building to various groups, and this has helped tremendously those who are struggling to get off drugs. There are too few programs for teenagers. And a lot of federal funding is available to pilot a program like this.

● Begin small groups. Other than a formal NA/AA group, small groups are another way to reach the addicted young person. In small groups, kids will talk honestly with each other about the difficulties that they face.

IT'S A SPIRITUAL PROBLEM

To fight drug and alcohol use, you must learn about the enemy you're fighting against. It's not just a physical war, but a spiritual one as well. Nothing takes the place of prayer for any young person lost in this battle.

● Go where they go. This will give you the heart of God for the young people. When our young people took a trip to Jerusalem, one night we went to Ben Yehuda Street in downtown Jerusalem, a busy street full of night life and lots of young people. Underneath a bank on the corner of a busy street, we set up a music team to sing songs of God's love to the people on the streets. As we set up, thinking we had found a suitable place to meet young people, we began to clean up the area. This area was full of broken bottles and the smell of urine. Where we were, unknown to us, was the place where many of the homeless drug-addicted youth of Israel "lived." As we sang, we felt the presence of God more in that place than in any of the other "holy" places we had seen earlier that day. We knew that we were literally where Jesus would have been if he were walking the streets of Israel today.

Being with the poor, needy, and wounded is the heart of God. Keep close to God's heart by going to the places where these young people are. This is where Jesus wants you to go.

● Target those areas with prayer. Begin by taking a small team of adults and some of your strong youth to the places where young people are struggling with drugs and alcohol. If you see them at the local parking lot, movie theater, or mall, notice them and take time to pray for them. If you're threatened by them, keep coming back. Don't be intimidated by those areas. Light is stronger than darkness.

● Realize that young people who struggle with addictions are precious to God. They're treasures. God has given you the answer and the power to help them through their struggles.

● Expect God to start opening doors for you to talk with these kids.

● Walk through those doors with caution. Be kind and accepting. Show your love and concern. Don't begin by sharing the gospel and preaching to these kids. They want love; they're not looking for religion. They usually aren't interested in the bigger questions of life, they just want to be loved and to feel good about themselves.

IT'S A HEART PROBLEM

When you minister to drug- and alcohol-abusing young people, you must see into their hearts. Once we had a young teenager who was really struggling with severe drug abuse. He came into the building, weeping. I asked him why he was high. He said, "I have to get high to forget all this pain." There's a deep sense of loneliness and woundedness in young people today. They often feel abandoned and rejected. Many don't have families that are together. Those who do may feel as if their families don't care much for them. They struggle with school, friends, and life. Many have chosen a slow suicide. All because they don't know that God deeply loves and cares for them.

● Get into their lives. There is nothing like an adult who is willing to get into the life of a young person. Today's generation of teenagers wants adults in their lives, but most don't know any adults with whom they can connect. If you can help them just by being there, this is the beginning of healing for many youth.

● Coordinate other adults with a heart for young people to begin a mentoring program with these kids.

● Help them with their families. One of the greatest gifts you can give a young person is to help restore his or her family. We have a young girl in the ministry who wasn't in a good relationship with her mom. We began to pray with her regarding this area. It seemed like an impossibility. Then one evening, the mother tried to end her life, taking too many pills because of a nasty divorce. We prayed for her, and the mother lived. The girl shared her love for God with her mom. The following week, her mother came to the youth meeting. It was a good service with lots of prayer. Her mother wept openly and gave her heart to the Lord. Today, although the mother and father are divorced, the daughter and the mother are fully restored.

Don't be afraid to help restore a family. This is also in the heart of God. Obviously there are some situations that can't be restored, but many young people, no matter how intense the problems, want some kind of restoration of relationship with their families. Sometimes having other adults in their lives is just enough to give them the support they need to make things right with their parents.

● When dealing with young people with substance abuse issues, look at their hearts and see the little children within them. Love them. Be committed to help them, and rescue them even if they don't appear to want it. Realize that God has placed you in their lives and that you're in a position to make a difference.

● Remember that God is the Great Shepherd who goes after the one sheep and leaves the ninety-nine. When you go after any young person who is struggling, and when you show God's love and hope, you'll always have God's heart with you as you go.

the greatest of these is love

Building Bridges to Teenage Moms

MARY SOMERVILLE • Director • Young Life's Mentor
Moms • Visalia, California

You are probably reading this chapter because you know a teenage mom and you feel compelled to reach out to her. My goal is to encourage you and give you some practical suggestions for this God-honoring task. If you're reading this chapter and you don't feel compelled to help teenage moms, I'm here to spur you on toward that end. Let me begin by saying it's best for mature women to reach out to teenage moms. They are best equipped to address her needs without complicating or confusing her life.

Look at the needs of a teenage mom. They're great in every area of her life—physically, socially, emotionally, intellectually, and spiritually.

Let's consider how we can address her physical needs. Her physical needs may include a place to live, food, or clothing. Perhaps her parents want her out of the house. The church can't just say, "Be warmed and fed." We must step in and meet real needs. My husband's family took in a young woman who had been turned out of her home. Her Christian parents in another state didn't want the stigma of their daughter having a baby outside marriage. She wanted to do things God's way, recognizing that she had sinned. She received love and care throughout the pregnancy in this Christlike family, and her life was spared for God's kingdom.

Look at her social needs. This young woman probably feels cut off from her peers. She may feel trapped and lonely. She must now think about the baby she is carrying. She is limited from many activities. She is tied down when the baby arrives. Her friends usually don't care to hang around her. She has no one to help shoulder the burden of her child. That is where a loving friend can come into her life and help with these deep needs.

Her emotional needs must be met. Teenage moms are going through an extremely emotional time of life. Having a baby is physically and emotionally draining. Lots of changes are taking place in her body and emotions. There has been a sexual relationship which she probably looked at as love. That "love relationship" may be stressed to the breaking point through the pregnancy. The boyfriend may bail out. This is a heartbreaking situation. If he remains in her life, they have a lot to work out. It can turn into a very turbulent time. Parental relationships may be very strained. The teenage mom needs a friend who can listen attentively and give hope and direction through loving biblical counsel.

The teenage mom has intellectual needs to be addressed. Is she going to be able to finish school? With the help and encouragement of her family or a friend, that is possible. She may need to find a job to support herself and her child. That also can be talked about and worked on together with a friend who wants to see her succeed in life.

The young mom has a need for information on how to care for her baby. Mothering is an overwhelming task, especially at such a young age. If she is from a dysfunctional family, she may have no good role models for raising a child. She may not know how to give and receive love or any of the other skills necessary for good child rearing.

The teenage mom has spiritual needs. She needs to experience the love and grace of Christ and know his forgiveness and new direction for her life. If she's caught in the trap of a promiscuous lifestyle, she needs to know about the liberating power of Christ. If she has experienced physical or sexual abuse, she needs the hope and comfort of the Scriptures.

LOVE IS THE BRIDGE

Following are the ingredients of true love from 1 Corinthians 13, along with some relevant examples of how each part can be used to build a bridge to teenage moms. Meditate on this passage and add to the list yourself.

LOVE IS PATIENT

Love for teenage moms is patient—it waits on God to work in their lives. It doesn't try to do the work of the Holy Spirit but prays and trusts God to work.

● Love is spelled T-I-M-E. Spend time with an individual teenage mom or in a small group. This tells her that you truly care about her. Spending time with her is your best way of winning the right to be heard. It's identifying with her where she is. It's going on her turf.

● Don't be nosy in pushing for details of her life. Wait for her to share as the relationship grows. Don't expect immediate closeness. You can wait until she is ready to share something. Wait for the trust to grow.

● Let her know you're deeply committed to her. You aren't bailing out. You're going to be there for her. There are no shortcuts to building a friendship. It involves lots of time.

● Pray devotedly for her to give her life to Christ, even when it seems impossible. Then simply wait for God to open her heart to him.

LOVE IS KIND

Love for teenage moms is kind—it looks for ways of showing kindness through words and deeds.

● Listen to her. Be sensitive to her feelings. Let her know you understand by the way you listen and seek to get involved in helping her find answers to her concerns.

● Take an interest in her pregnancy. Talk about your own pregnancy if you've experienced one. Give her tips you learned firsthand or from things you've picked up through reading.

● Offer to be her birth coach. This is a real bonding time. If she has someone else, you can offer to be in the waiting room praying for her as she is in labor. The interest and support is so meaningful at this important time in her life.

● Show interest in her baby. In some cases her family hasn't been celebrating the child because of the conditions of the birth. However, as you reach out, you know God can use this child for good. This child is not an accident. God designed this child and placed him or her in the mother's womb. She made the right decision not to end this baby's life with an abortion. Now she needs help and encouragement in her pregnancy and in raising the child. This can serve as the bridge to a relationship with Christ which will meet her greatest needs.

- Give her a baby shower. If she is a non-Christian, this a good way for you to point her to Christ through a heavy dose of love as you and your friends shower her with gifts and loving wishes. If she is a Christian, she should be forgiven and supported in this way as she enters her new role as a mother.

- Take pictures of her and her baby. This shows interest in her child and gives them a record of your times together.

- Remembering her birthday and the birthday of her child is important. Doing things together on holidays is another way of showing interest. Help her make good memories with her child.

- Baby-sit on prearranged occasions. She will trust you with the care of her baby because you've built a strong bridge of friendship.

- Have fun together. Teenage moms have the huge responsibility of raising a child. They need opportunities to have fun. As you do fun things together, barriers are broken down. Fun things might include doing a craft together. It might mean going to the park for a picnic, making popcorn and watching a video, going to the mall and window shopping, or visiting a mutual friend.

- Include her in your family. The love expressed by the other members of your family only deepens the love you have expressed to her. This provides her with a laboratory of family relationships in which she'll observe how you treat your husband and children.

- Reach out to her boyfriend and the father of her baby. He is important in her life and in the life of her child. (Many times he's out of the picture, but if he's still in her life, it's very important to reach out and build a bridge to him as well.) Include him in family times, dinner, or other activities. Have a man reach out to him, one-on-one if possible.

- If she commits her life to Christ and her boyfriend hasn't, discourage her from marrying him and encourage her to break off the relationship. It is one of the kindest things you can do to spare her from years of being married to a non-Christian.

- Do extra loving things for her. Send her a card for no reason but to say, "I love you." Give her a phone call to say, "Hi, how are you doing?" Make a special meal with foods she especially likes. Remember her on her birthday with balloons and a cake. There are so many ways to say, "You are special to me." A hug can be very important to a gal who needs a personal touch that says, "I care."

LOVE DOES NOT ENVY

Love for teenage moms does not envy—it does not think, "I am the only one that can work with that girl to bring her to Christ."

● Don't be possessive of the teenage mom. Get others involved.

● Accept the fact that she may not naturally come to you first for advice. Once again, be patient and freely offer the advice when she asks.

● Ask the mother of the teenage mom for permission to reach out and minister to her daughter. You want her to know that you aren't trying to steal her place. Most Christian mothers will appreciate sharing the load with another concerned Christlike woman. If her mother isn't a Christian, this is a great chance to reach out to her and the rest of the family. They need the gospel and probably are hurting as well. If the mother hesitates to involve you in her daughter's life, you may need to pull back and respect her wishes.

LOVE DOES NOT BOAST

Love for teenage moms does not boast—but keeps in mind that everything that is accomplished is by God's power and for his glory.

● Don't flaunt your possessions, family, good track record, or anything else. Your job is not to impress her, but to love her.

● Don't spend a lot of money. Putting emphasis on material things detracts from the focus of the friendship. When giving small gifts, give meaningful gifts such as children's books, Christian musical tapes and videos for the child, things to spur her on in her walk with Christ, and tools to encourage her child-rearing skills.

LOVE IS NOT PROUD

Love for teenage moms is not proud—it does not allow one to think of herself as better than her teenager.

● Keep a humble spirit. It is only by God's grace that you are not in her situation. Have the mind of Christ who went to the extent of dying the death of a criminal for us (Philippians 2:8).

● Be vulnerable. Don't present a perfect image of yourself. Everyone struggles and deals with sin. She will gain hope as she sees the reality that everyone needs God's help. She is not unique in her needs. Realize that you can't begin to solve all her problems but you can search the Scriptures for God's solutions and help her see his way to live.

- Share your own past hurts or difficulties you've encountered. Her problems are common, and they have common solutions. God helped you through your hard situations, and he will also be faithful to see her through her difficulties.

LOVE IS NOT RUDE

Love for teenage moms is not rude—it is respectful and caring.

- Don't think you have to dress like her or talk like her or like her style of music or all the things she admires. Many of the things she thinks are cool are actually very unbecoming to a Christian. Don't conform. You're different. You don't have to be alike. Love will bridge the gap. Accept her as she is and seek to be her friend with no strings attached. As Christ works in her life, she'll see the unattractiveness of these things and admire the Christlike, gentle, and quiet spirit that you exude.

LOVE IS NOT SELF-SEEKING

Love for teenage moms is not self-seeking—it comes to serve, not to be served.

- It has been said that "you know you are a true servant when you are treated like one and you don't mind."

- Don't expect her to show appreciation, or even to say "thank you."

- Look for ways to serve her by meeting her physical, social, emotional, intellectual, and spiritual needs. You can seek to minister to her in each area of her life. God desires to care for people through us (James 2:14-18).

LOVE IS NOT EASILY ANGERED

Love for teenage moms is not easily angered—instead of getting upset, it gives up expectations to God and trusts him through disappointments, patiently bearing up under them.

- Love her when she doesn't seem to reciprocate at all. "If you love those who love you, what reward will you get? Are not even the tax collectors doing that?" (Matthew 5:46). You must expect the relationship to be tested. She probably has been let down by many people and will expect you to also give up on her or fail her. She will test you to see if you really do love her and will not give up on her.

- When you are tempted to be angry with her, instead pray for her (Matthew 5:44).

- When she treats you disrespectfully, go the extra mile to respect her and find a way to serve her further (Matthew 5:38-42). Return good for evil (Romans 12:17-21).

LOVE KEEPS NO RECORD OF WRONGS

Love for teenage moms does not keep a record of wrongs—it does not keep score on the number of times it has been let down.

● Your forgiveness must be limitless. She may sin against you not just seven times, but seventy times seven, and you must willingly forgive, remembering how much you have been forgiven by a holy God (Matthew 18:21-35).

LOVE DOES NOT DELIGHT IN EVIL

Love for teenage moms does not delight in evil—when a young woman continues to practice sin, grieve and seek to restore her.

● There may be many things a teenage mom does that are sinful and cannot be encouraged. Use these sins in her life to point her to her need for the Savior. Then look for the good things that can be nourished.

● Be honest. She'll be expecting you to hold up a biblical standard. Don't compromise truth to make a friend—this is seeking your own interests more than hers. Speak the truth in love. She'll respect you for it in the end.

LOVE REJOICES WITH THE TRUTH

Love for teenage moms rejoices with the truth—when your beloved teenage mom obeys God's Word or even grows in acceptance of practical truths, have a party!

● Pick up on her interests and dreams. Observe her. Show interest in her special abilities. Encourage her to develop skills that you notice. For instance, if she is interested in the medical field and shows aptitude for math and science, help her explore career options available to her. Bring her articles relating to the medical field. Help her to meet people in the field. Find out more about it yourself so you can talk knowledgeably with her. If she has no goals or dreams, help her find some. Make some suggestions of what you see God using her to accomplish with his enabling.

● Capitalize on her strengths. For instance, if she's a good caregiver to her baby, she could be encouraged to go into some form of working with children. Let her know that she has great potential with God's help. Praise her for her strengths. "You did great!" "You made me proud." "Wow, that was awesome!" Affirming words can make a real difference in your teenage mom's life. You must look for opportunities to uplift and give hope for the future.

● She will need to be discipled in many practical areas of her life. Talk about baby care to stimulate her child's development, such as through spending time rocking and singing to her child and then reading to him or her, and playing with the child as he or she gets older. If you're a young mom, you'll be modeling all these things.

- The church is the pillar and support of the truth. Encourage your teenage-mom friend to become involved in a church so she can learn and grow in the truth.

- Include her in your church/women's ministry/Bible study circle of friends. She'll experience the love of all of these people. You'll be bringing her in and encouraging them to reach out to her as well. You may need to stay with her baby in the church nursery the first few times. You may need to pick her up and take her with you to each of the functions and sit with her. She'll need the one-on-one commitment.

- Find out if she's interested in attending the youth group at your church. Many times teenage moms feel out of place with people their own age or younger because they're now moms with different responsibilities and interests. If she feels comfortable in the group, it's a good place for her to plug in. If not, perhaps she could get involved in another small-group Bible study or cell group with families and people of all ages.

- Take her to MOPS (Mothers of Preschoolers) meetings if there is a chapter in your area. Their activities are geared for young mothers, with a Christian focus.

- Become a mentor with Young Life's Mentor Moms, which is a program that matches teenage moms with Christian women in a mentoring relationship. Or start a program yourself. (*Mentor Moms: A Handbook for Mentoring Teen Mothers* is available from the Young Life Service Center, (719) 381-1800.)

LOVE ALWAYS PROTECTS, ALWAYS TRUSTS, ALWAYS HOPES, ALWAYS PERSEVERES

- **Love for a teenage mom always protects**—it seeks to shield and defend her against the inroads of sin in her life.

- **Love for teenage moms always trusts**—when she puts her trust in Jesus, when she says she wants to change, when she says she's sorry for the broken appointment, when she says she was hurt by your pride.

- **Love for teenage moms hopes all things**—that God can do great things and give her a hope and a future through the power of his Spirit working in her.

- **Love for teenage moms perseveres through all things**—broken appointments, lack of appreciation, lack of interest in Jesus, rejection, and betrayal. It never, never gives up!

LOVE NEVER FAILS

Love for teenage moms never fails—it always accomplishes the purpose for which God gives it: to draw young women to Jesus. God's love never fails. Therefore you must never stop loving a girl through Christ's love flowing through you. Remember, God never gave up on you!

"And now these three remain: faith, hope and love. But the greatest of these is love" (1 Corinthians 13:13).

special needs, special gifts

Ministering to Youth With Disabilities

JULIE MEIKLEJOHN · General Director · Camp Hope ·
Fort Collins, Colorado

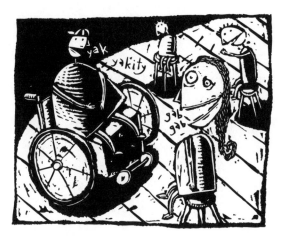

"**A** tool unto itself is of little importance, but placed in the proper hands it can create a masterpiece."

This quote, from the book *Friendship Unlimited* by Joni Eareckson Tada, effectively expresses the place youth with disabilities should have within your youth group.

You may have never been near a person with a disability, or you may understand living with a disability on an intimate level. Either way, the prospect of working closely with a youth group member with disabilities may seem an intimidating prospect—one which raises more questions than it answers. "What if I say the wrong thing?" "How should I treat him?" "What if I don't know how to meet her needs?" "What if he says or does something strange or inappropriate?"

"How can I help the other members of my group understand and respect her?"

Youth with disabilities need love and acceptance—both from you and from the other members of your youth group—just as much as any "normal" youth group member. They also have many gifts to give. Many people with mental disabilities have the ability to look beyond outer appearances and reach out in genuine love to all kinds of people. Those with physical disabilities can provide an inspiring example to those with more able bodies. A disability does not mean diminished ability, it just means different ability.

The most important thing to remember in working with people with disabilities is to always treat them with respect and compassion. They may take a little extra time to do things, or they may need a little extra help, but they can both gain much from and give much to the body of Christ.

"Whatever you did for one of the least of these brothers of mine, you did for me" (Matthew 25:40b).

● All God's children are given spiritual gifts to use in his service, even those with the most profound disabilities. Help the members of your youth group discover their own and each other's spiritual gifts. Use 1 Corinthians 12 as a starting place, and discuss the different types of spiritual gifts people may have. You may even want to use a spiritual gifts survey.

● Institute a youth leadership team, in which youth help make decisions and plans for the youth group as a whole. Try to include youth with disabilities in planning and decision-making as much as possible.

● Above all, youth group members who have disabilities want to be treated just like everyone else. Strive not to single them out or embarrass them by focusing on the ways in which they are different.

● Encourage compassion and sensitivity in all group members by finding or creating opportunities for them to help people with many different needs. For example, your group might lead vacation Bible school for economically disadvantaged children or work on a house with Habitat for Humanity. Do a Bible study on 2 Corinthians 1:3-4 to help youth group members understand that God enables them to help others who have burdens much greater than their own.

● Able-bodied people may not be aware of the physical barriers those with physical disabilities face constantly, limiting their full participation in some activities. Go through your church, particularly the rooms in which the youth group spends most of its time, and try to visualize what it would be like for a person with disabilities. Note narrow doorways, stairways without alternate routes, and other possible difficulties or hazards. Work to remove or change any physical barriers to full participation.

● Allow youth with disabilities to participate fully in all youth group activities by modifying activities on an individual basis only when it's absolutely necessary.

● Ask youth group members who have disabilities (if they're receptive to the idea) to help "teach" the group the best ways to work and interact with those with disabilities, highlighting especially the ways they would like to be treated. An excellent resource is the book *Friendship Unlimited* by Joni Eareckson Tada.

● Be sure to be aware of, and prepared to help with, any special-care needs a youth group member with disabilities may have, especially if he or she will be away from home for an extended period of time, such as at a retreat.

● Educate yourself as well as the rest of your youth group. Do some research about the type of disability a youth group member has. This information may help you to work with and care for him or her more effectively.

● Examine your own views of disabilities and people who have them. Take a few minutes to answer the following questions as honestly as possible: Do you feel pity? Do you think all people with disabilities have "hearts of gold" and should be constantly appreciative of what everyone is doing for them? Do you believe it's best to leave people with disabilities alone to "be with their own kind"? Do you view them as "projects"? Do you feel afraid of people with disabilities? If so, why? Do you see people with disabilities as being sick? Imagine you became disabled today. How do you think you would respond?

● Search Scripture to discover God's view of disabilities. A few passages to start with are Exodus 4:11; 2 Samuel 9; Psalm 139:13-16; Isaiah 35:1-6; Lamentations 3:32, 38; Romans 8:28; 2 Corinthians 4:7-12; and 1 Thessalonians 5:18.

● Strive to model and encourage compassionate, respectful behavior among youth group members by following these guidelines:

■ Ask a person with disabilities if he or she needs your help and how you can help, rather than just assuming the person needs or wants your help.

■ Wheelchairs, crutches, walkers, and canes are an extension of the person who uses them. They are the person's mode of transportation. Refrain from sitting in wheelchairs or using such equipment without first asking permission from the owner.

■ Treat a person with disabilities as you would any other person. Don't stereotype him or her.

■ Be kind and considerate. Don't belittle or talk down to a person with disabilities. Sit at the same eye level as the person while engaged in conversation. Never pat a person with disabilities on the head.

■ Be patient. People with disabilities often take more time to express themselves.

■ Greet a person with visual impairments by identifying yourself. Do not lead the person; allow him or her to hold onto your arm instead.

■ When talking to a person with a hearing impairment, face the light and speak calmly and slowly. Use gestures and write notes as appropriate.

■ Don't ask questions about a person's disability unless it seems appropriate. Use common sense and sensitivity.

■ Avoid labeling people with disabilities. Identify them as people first (for example, "the girl who is deaf").

■ Don't assume a youth group member with disabilities can't participate. Emphasize the abilities of each person.

- Maintain clear, consistent standards for youth group behavior.
- Help a person with mental disabilities by presenting simple, clear instructions, breaking down activities into small steps, and giving lots of positive feedback.

● As you and the members of your youth group strive to fully accept and include persons of varying abilities, you may want to use this version of the Beatitudes for inspiration:

"Blessed are you who take the time to listen to difficult speech, for you help me to know that if I persevere I can be understood.

"Blessed are you who never bid me to 'hurry up' and take my tasks from me and do them for me; for often I need time rather than help.

"Blessed are you who stand beside me as I enter new and untried ventures, for my failures will be outweighed by the times I surprise myself and you.

"Blessed are you who ask for my help, for my greatest need is to be needed.

"Blessed are you who understand that it is difficult for me to put my thoughts into words.

"Blessed are you who encourage me with a smile to try once more.

"Blessed are you who never remind me that today I asked the same question two times.

"Blessed are you who respect me and love me as I am, just as I am, and not like you wish I were."

(Anonymous, from *Friendship Unlimited* by Joni Eareckson Tada)

● Study the story of the four men lowering their friend through the roof to see Jesus (Mark 2:1-12), and discuss the nature of true friendship and the ways in which compassion sometimes requires creative solutions to problems.

● Sometimes those with disabilities may not have come to terms with their disabilities. Manifest true compassion by crying with those who cry (Romans 12:15), allowing the angry to express anger, giving the doubtful room for doubt, and dedicating yourself to consistent involvement.

● For those with more involved disabilities, you may want to use a buddy system, in which able-bodied youth group members volunteer to "come alongside" those with disabilities, offering friendship and help and encouragement when it's needed.

● Host a "disability awareness" event for the members of your church. Ask all members of your youth group to help present the practical information in this chapter and other resources in creative, active ways.

● Affirm youth group members with disabilities (and able-bodied youth group members as well!) using the following formula:

1. State the behavior you have actually observed. For example, you might say, "David, I saw you showing Jake, the new guy, around this morning."

2. Mention a few details about what you saw. For example, you might say, "You showed him where we meet and told him all about our Wednesday night Bible studies and the trips we go on."

3. Explain the importance or meaning of your observation. For example, you might say, "That shows what real friendship is."

● Make your group a place where people with disabilities feel safe and accepted by making a conscious, continual effort to foster solid relationships and an atmosphere of trust among all group members.

● Before going on a trip with your youth group, determine how accessible facilities are ahead of time to avoid embarrassing a group member with disabilities.

● Be aware of the language you use. For example, if one of your group members uses a wheelchair, you might not want to ask members to stand to indicate their votes in an activity.

● Group members with disabilities may have more trouble making friends than their able-bodied counterparts. Encourage friendships by doing plenty of activities that require mingling.

international connections

Ministering to Foreign Exchange Students in American High Schools

ANDY FLETCHER • Deputy Director • Young Life's International Schools Ministry • Colorado Springs, Colorado

ens of thousands of foreign exchange students arrive on American shores every fall for their one-year experience in a U.S. high school. They land full of excitement about improving their English, making friends with U.S. kids, experiencing U.S. culture, food, and leisure activities. They want to see America—the cities, the parks, the canyons, the mountains, and the beaches. They want to meet Americans, eat American food, learn the slang, listen to the music, and watch the movies.

They're nervous about living with an American family, but excited. It's their chance to experience everything they're looking forward to.

They come from countries literally all over the planet—from Asia, from Middle Eastern countries, from nations in the former Soviet bloc, from the 10-40 Window (a rectangular area 10 to 40 degrees north latitude of the Equator. It is a belt of nations that, though predominantly Muslim, also hosts a number of other religions, including: Buddhist, Hindu, Jewish, Zoroastrian, Confucian, and all the others).

They clearly represent a chance for American Christians to be foreign missionaries without leaving the comfort of their own beds and homes—the Great Commission commands us to go into all the world, and yet every fall in each of our cities and high schools, all the world has come to us.

What then has generally been our reaction? Mixed, at best. Although many times Christian families will take exchange students into their homes and use that time to expose them gently to the gospel, most American Christians, like Americans at large, don't really know what to do. We're awkward around kids from different parts of the world. We don't know what questions to ask, what to talk about, how to relate. In addition, U.S. high school students, especially in the upper two or three grades, have a full quiver of friends. Since making friends with people from overseas is hard, it's an easy thing to avoid.

Thus exchange students frequently find themselves lonely and isolated in their high schools. Some will join clubs and teams, but many more will wander the halls for the year, foreign and solitary islands alone in the midst of the chaotic life of a high school.

Most exchange students come from places where public transportation is efficient and normative, only to arrive in American communities where most public transportation is dirty, inefficient, and undependable, and where it may not be at all safe for high school kids, especially girls, to wander around on their own. They are not legal drivers in their own countries and are not allowed to get drivers' licenses in this one. They also are likely to be from places which are much safer in terms of the threat of crime, so they're accustomed to being much more free and independent, able to get around easily without a car or fear for their personal safety. Their host families do their best to shuttle them around, but quickly it grows tiring, and the exchange students find themselves home alone.

They're also eager to see America, that is, the historic sights, scenery, theme parks, national parks, and the other wonders we sometimes take for granted. There are local sights to see in most communities, and others at greater distances. Again, the host families try mightily to take them everywhere, but Americans are busy, with commitments in all directions. It's hard to keep an eager exchange student busy all the time.

It's especially hard when one considers the character and circumstances of many of these students. Many have finished their education and have no need of an American diploma. The comparable curricula in many countries are quite different from that in the United States, so the students may be significantly ahead of their American peers, and thus bored in class.

However, they tend to be bright and well-motivated, and they share a quality that is almost universal—they love to discuss the great questions of life, including spirituality and God.

CASE STUDY:

Young Life in Colorado Springs developed an outreach ministry to foreign exchange students at the local schools. We met them at a Rotary luncheon, got their names, countries, and local addresses, and put them in a database. We sponsored monthly events designed specifically for them, including a one-day trip to Denver, a ski trip in the Rockies, a service project to a Navajo reservation, and so on. Several of the volunteers spent significant time building relationships with some of the kids. Eventually, the ministry transitioned into Young Life staff and interns getting the exchange students involved in club ministry so they would meet American students from their own host schools. A great American experience was coupled with a chance to hear the gospel.

We also spent significant amounts of time in casual discussion. A weekend in a cabin, deluged by torrential rains, was spent entirely in conversation and discussions. It was an unusual time of sharing on matters of faith and belief.

FIND A WAY TO MEET THEM

- Our local Rotary Club, under the urging of a Young Life staff person who is a longtime member, puts on a welcoming luncheon in the early fall to which all of the exchange students in town are invited. Young Life staff members and interns volunteer to pick up the kids from their schools and sit at the various tables with them. A short talk is given on some of the events Young Life offers during the year. A church can do likewise, using volunteers. It might be wise to involve several church youth pastors in the event.

- Your student leaders at the schools can easily meet the exchange students in their schools, introduce you to them, and invite them to your events.

- You might volunteer to set up, or be a part of, a welcome program for them at the school, to ease their assimilation into school life. You can tell them about all aspects of school life, have representatives from the various teams and clubs make short presentations, and perhaps even get student helpers to be "forex buddies" for the first couple of weeks. You could also give them an overview of what your town is like, perhaps give them free certificates to ice-cream shops, skating rinks, movie theaters, and so on. Another help would be to familiarize them with available forms of transportation, and maybe offer a short tour of the hot spots in town such as malls and so on.

- You may be able to meet them by building relationships with representatives from the various foreign exchange organizations. Caution: These folks are sometimes nervous about religious organizations or people with church or parachurch connections.

- Some of the families in your church may be host families, or can be encouraged to become host families. This is a natural way to get exchange students involved. You might also host one yourself.

TRY TO BUILD RELATIONSHIPS

- Get to know them through your student leaders.
- Offer them rides to and from places (such as the mall and the school).
- Plan special trips to local or regional tourist sights.
- Invite them to spend time with your family (dinners, weekend trips, and so on).
- Offer to help with day-to-day needs (such as shopping).
- Invite them on ski trips, beach trips, bike trips, and so on.
- Invite them on service projects—this is a great tool.

- Invite them to (and create if necessary) outreach events.

- Get involved in their lives and school activities.

- Help them with their English.

- Invite them just to spend time with you in town. What seems like an ordinary boring day to you can be a fascinating cultural experience for a foreign student.

- Invite them to church. Again, this is a cultural experience for them in the same way it would be for you if you went to a Buddhist temple.

- Invite them for American holiday celebrations, especially Christmas and Easter.

- Take them to local parades, festivals, county and state fairs, rodeos, and other typically American events.

- If you have a group from one country (Germany, for example), do a little research into its holidays and invite them to celebrate one with you. You might enlist their help in planning it (since they know better than you what to do).

- Be ready for the hard questions about faith and religion, and don't make the mistake of giving pat, rote answers. These kids will challenge your understanding of your faith in tough ways. If you don't meet them halfway, you will lose them.

- After you discover the countries of origin, do a little homework. Read up on the various countries—about recent history and current events.

- Also find out how the United States has been involved in their countries' histories. Recognize that it's not always useful spiritually to be too defensive about certain unfortunate U.S. actions around the world, certainly not out of ignorance.

- Be aware of the various religious expressions of faith in their countries and know something about them—it's more tactically useful to find something positive in their faith and affirm its similarity to Christian doctrine than to look for the negatives.

- To enable smooth conversations, it might be useful to have some questions in mind in advance of a first meeting, just questions about who they are and where they're from—prepare your student leaders as well. It may be necessary for you to alter your normal conversation style—you may need to speak somewhat more slowly and to avoid too many idioms and slang. However, they want to learn all the slang, so if you do use it and they don't get it, explain it to them. Caution: Don't talk to them as though they are stupid or deaf. Just be sensitive to their needs.

- Be aware of how strategic an opportunity this is—have, and give your kids, a "10-40" vision. As you may know, a neglected and sensitive area of the world on which the U.S. missions community is focused is that swath of countries lying between 10 and 40 degrees north latitude. It includes North Africa and the Middle East, Pakistan, India, and much of Asia. These are the countries where there is much resistance to the gospel and little hospitality offered to missionaries—these are Muslim, Buddhist, and Hindu nations where Christians can be, and often are, persecuted for their faith. When kids leave these countries to become foreign exchange students and then have life-changing encounters with Christ, they return to countries with few local Christians. (It may be necessary for you to talk to these kids about some of the real and dangerous difficulties they may face upon their return—you may want to do a little research to find out how best to deal with the issue.)

  This ministry is strategic for all parts of the world, of course—Western Europe, where the faith has been struggling for generations; Latin America, where a more cultural faith can easily blossom into a personal relationship with Christ; and so on. Your kids have a chance to be missionaries to the world while never leaving their own schools.

- Be ready for a long process of evangelism—kids may be angry and may accuse you of manipulation and brainwashing.

- Exchange students love small-group discussions. Teach more than preach, talk more than teach, ask more than talk, listen more than ask, pray more than anything, and model the love and compassion of Christ.

VOLUNTEERS

One challenging aspect of outreach to foreign exchange students is finding willing volunteers. It's not only American teens who are unsure about how to act around foreigners; American adults are as well. Here are some hints:

Be wise in your recruiting. You will find your best volunteers from among the following types of people, looking of course for committed Christians:

- Former missionaries and missionary kids (check with churches and missions agencies in your town)

- Families who have lived overseas while working for multinational businesses and diplomatic agencies (check with multinational corporations with offices in your town)

- Naturalized American citizens from other countries (check with local churches)

- Foreign language students in high schools, especially in the more advanced levels (probably from among the kids you know, or check with any teachers you might know)

- Foreign language teachers in schools (again, probably people you know, or you can check with other churches)

- Foreign language students from local colleges (check with on-campus Christian ministries, campus chaplains, college departments in nearby churches)

- College students from other countries (check with foreign student organizations on campus)

- College students who have had a year abroad

- Former American foreign exchange students (check with foreign exchange programs in town)

- American college students who lived overseas for some of their secondary education studying in international schools (they're hard to find—maybe run an ad in the college newspaper)

Even if you can find volunteers from among the ranks of these types of people, you may still need to offer some hints on how to talk to foreign exchange students. Here are some resources for opening conversations:

- *The World at Your Door* by Phillips and Norsworthy (Bethany House), pages 92-98. This includes lists of questions on topics such as someone's country, city or village, house and family, language and customs, sociology, family life, gender roles, recreation, transportation, education, food, and faith.

- For small-group questions, excellent resources are *The Book of Questions* (non-Christian) by Gregory Stock (Workman), and several Christian offerings from Youth Specialties: *What If…?, Would You Rather…?,* and *Have You Ever…?*

- To deal with issues of cultural sensitivity, *The World at Your Door* offers some excellent help. Some of the following books are also good: *Learning About Theology From the Third World,* William Dyrness (Zondervan), *How Does America Hear the Gospel,* William Dyrness (Eerdmans), and *Ministering Cross-Culturally,* Lingenfelter/Mayers (Baker).

reaching beyond the rage

Connecting With Youth Who Have Anger Issues

DR. SCOTT J. LARSON • President • Straight Ahead
Ministries • Westboro, Massachusetts

A nger—everybody has it, but it just seems to ooze from some kids. You're never quite sure when they may erupt, but after being blasted a few times, you begin to feel like you're walking on eggshells whenever you're around them. In fact, they seem to go beyond just being angry to being filled with rage.

Even the Bible seems to distinguish between the two. Anger is a normal emotion, not sinful in itself. That's why the Apostle Paul and the psalmist could say, "In your anger do not sin" (Ephesians 4:26). Jesus himself displayed anger when he drove the money-changers out of the temple (John 2:15), and God at various times acts out of his anger toward sin, evidenced by the flood and his outrage at the children of Israel worshipping a golden calf.

Sometimes anger can be productive, as with Martin Luther King, Jr., whose anger toward racism drove him to launch the civil rights movement of the 1960s.

But rage is altogether different. It's impossible to be filled with rage and still remain pure because rage controls us. Scripture always lists rage along with other sinful acts, such as sexual immorality, debauchery, idolatry, witchcraft, hatred, discord, jealousy, selfish ambition, drunkenness, malice, bitterness, slander, and filthy language (Galatians 5:19-20; Ephesians 4:31; and Colossians 3:8).

The problem for the rage-filled teenager is that he or she is unable to turn it off as a mere act of the will. Unlike normal anger, rage almost always erupts into destructive acts such as screaming, cursing, breaking objects, or hitting. When we ask kids in detention centers to estimate the level of their anger on a thermometer from zero to ten, most say it never goes below seven or eight, even in the best of times. As they carry around their fury, strapped on like short-fused dynamite, they're danger zones waiting to be crossed. A slight provocation, such as being disrespected on the street by a peer or corrected by a teacher in school, triggers an explosion. When we ask kids how many of them committed their crimes when they were at "ten," the majority raise their hands (Scott Larson, *At Risk: Bringing Hope to Hurting Teenagers*).

Where does all this rage come from? Often from experiencing rejection from close family members at an early age. For example, I once asked kids in a detention center Bible study how many had experienced rejection while growing up. Out of twelve kids in the group, five relayed stories of how someone close to them had tried to seriously hurt them when they were young. It's not surprising that anger is the driving emotion present in our detention centers and prisons today—but not only there; our churches and youth groups are filled with angry kids as well.

For some, anger is like a drug. It's what motivates and keeps them going. It gives them a reason for living, even though it's twisted. It helps them do things they never could do in the absence of such a powerful stimulus. For teenage gangs, anger and the desire for revenge is often the glue that holds them together. When we propose they let go of their anger, choosing instead to forgive, one can understand how this might be very threatening to an angry young person. But on the following pages are some ideas for helping teenagers begin that process of letting go.

- Help kids identify the cause of their anger. Most kids are angry for a reason. Some anger is the result of feelings of failure, disapproval, or frustration. Other times it comes from a sense of abandonment, betrayal, or alienation. Still other angry kids feel mostly deprived, hurt, or fearful. But if a teenager doesn't understand where the anger is coming from, he or she is unlikely to be able to deal with it. The young person likely will go through life struggling with anger but feeling powerless to change it. Kids like this need help in identifying where their anger is coming from.

- Build trust. Young people will not open up about the deep hurts in their lives with someone they don't trust. Staying with a them over the long haul is part of earning that trust, so when they're ready to talk about the past, you're there to process that with them. Then you can help them understand where their anger is coming from and how to appropriately address it.

- Model Christlike acceptance. If rejection is the root cause of most deep-seated anger, then it stands to reason that acceptance is at least part of the cure. I'm not talking about the bland "I accept you as you are," which is closer to apathy and indifference. But rather, the kind of acceptance that God extends toward us, whereby we confront their destructive behavior while still upholding their dignity as valuable and worthwhile people.

  When young people have someone who knows them at their worst yet still loves and accepts them, they possess a rare jewel.

- Expect sabotage. Youth who are angry tend to sabotage relationships with people who try to get close to them, figuring, "You're probably going to hurt me like everyone else has, so I'll hurt you first before you get a chance." They go through life longing for significant relationships, but being deathly afraid of them at the same time.

  The deeper the relationship develops, the more fearful they become. As one of the boys who lived in our home once said to me, "You're in a 'no-win' situation, Scott. You represent a father figure to us, and most of us hate our fathers. So we're naturally going to hate you, too, for awhile."

- Stick with them. Angry kids require adults who will stay with them long enough to repair their distorted parental image. It takes adults who are very secure in their own identity in Christ to unconditionally love kids through this difficult period; people who realize that the attacks aren't personal, but represent a lifetime of rejection. But having such relationships opens young people to being able to trust others as well. And as a result, the anger thermometer can begin to drop a couple of notches.

● Avoid speaking negatively about a young person's parents. Even when it seems clear that a teenager's mother or father is to blame, the parents are still the parents. And that parental bond is so strong that our negative words only put the young person in the awkward position of having to oppose us in order to defend the parent. If a person asks for your opinion, it's best to say something like "I know your mother loves you very much, it's just that she seems to have situations in her life right now that make it impossible for her to be all she wants and needs to be for you."

There is a very fine line between love and hate toward even an abusive parent. One of our staff recalls being at a campfire with a group of troubled boys toward the end of a ten-day wilderness trip when he asked, "What do you guys think of your fathers?"

The first one to speak spewed angrily, "I hate my father!" The mood grew more hostile as each one shared, until the very last boy spoke. "You know, I really love my father. I've never met him. But I really love him." One by one, each told similar stories of how they, too, love their fathers.

It illustrates just how important parents are, and how conflicted our views of them can be. It also shows why we must never speak ill of others' parents in their presence, no matter how poorly we think they've done.

● Teach about anger from the Scriptures. Anger is an important theme in the Scriptures, mentioned over seven hundred times. Yet most young people have no idea what the Bible really says about anger. Some think we're just not supposed to get mad. Or they may be confused about the difference between healthy anger and the seething rage that overtakes us. Kids need help in understanding God's perspective on anger, as well as receiving tools to help them deal with it positively. At the end of this chapter is one sample youth meeting on the general topic of anger.

● Teach anger-management techniques. While it's never healthy to stuff anger, neither is it healthy to immediately respond out of emotion. Proverbs 29:11 says, "A fool gives full vent to his anger, but a wise man keeps himself under control." There are many ways to defuse anger until a later point when the root causes of that anger can be dealt with appropriately.

James gives invaluable advice when he says, "Everyone should be quick to listen, slow to speak and slow to become angry" (James 1:19b). It can be helpful to count to ten before speaking or to simply say, "I'm not going to respond to that right now because I'm too angry," and then walk away. Going jogging, screaming into a pillow, or hitting a punching bag can release some of the immediate tension created by anger.

● Teach kids to deal with anger. One should never assume that anger will just disappear if we simply ignore it. That's why Paul insists, "Do not let the sun go down while you are still angry" (Ephesians 4:26b). As an old Latin proverb says, "He who goes angry to bed has the devil for a bedfellow." We must help kids learn to face their anger and work toward healthy resolution while they're still moldable and they haven't become ensnared in a lifestyle of un-resolved anger and bitterness.

● Point out the small successes kids do achieve. Nobody learns new skills overnight, and the same is true in dealing with anger. Rather than always feeling the guilt of failed attempts, kids need encouragement when they're able to *not* blow up in the face of disappointment or confrontation. They need someone who will be quick to point out when they do things right, not just when they fail. An old rule of thumb says kids need to hear seven posi-tive statements about themselves for every negative one.

● Build confidence. As kids begin to recognize the value of "holding their tongue" or "not letting the sun go down on their anger," they'll gain confi-dence for new challenges that may come their way.

● Recognize how anger begets anger. Kids have a way of exposing the worst in us, but angry kids don't leave a single stone unturned. Their anger tends to bring your own anger issues to the surface like almost nothing else. Yet when we respond to their anger with anger, situations quickly degenerate from bad to worse.

● Control your own anger. Proverbs 15:1 states, "A gentle answer turns away wrath, but a harsh word stirs up anger." Responding with gentleness requires us to be in touch with our own unresolved anger. And being transparent about our anger—not just the anger from twenty years ago, but our current strug-gles—can be very helpful for angry teens; then we aren't merely preaching to them, but sharing our own journey from rage to restfulness. This gives them hope for the same. It also illustrates how Christians appropriately deal with anger so that when they encounter it, they'll know what to do and not just con-clude, "I must not be a very good Christian, or I wouldn't be feeling this way."

● Help kids move toward forgiveness. "Forgiveness holds more promise for aid-ing an effective resolution to the problem of chronic anger than any other therapeutic intervention" (Les Parrott III, *Helping the Struggling Adolescent*), But forgiveness usually is the furthest thing from the mind of a rage-filled young person. Rather than trying to point out how the offender deserves forgiveness, emphasize the toll that harbored bitterness is taking on the teenager.

- Point them toward Christ. Forgiveness isn't a human trait; it's divine in nature. Thus, the first step in true forgiveness may be simply praying, "Lord, help me to at least be *willing* to forgive." Then in time one can move to "Lord, I need your strength to forgive this person. I know you want me to, but I can't do it on my own."

- Emphasize forgiveness as a process. Feelings of forgiveness may not come immediately, but when we're willing to take *steps of faith* to forgive, we can be assured of God's faithfulness to begin freeing us from the cancer of hatred.

- Know when to refer. Sometimes there are destructive physical consequences to a young person's chronic anger, such as ulcers, skin rashes, grinding teeth, high blood pressure, or clenched jaws (Les Parrott III, *Helping the Struggling Adolescent*). In other cases, the teenager's life or the life of another may be endangered because of the degree of rage present in his or her life. In this case it should be clear that normal interventions aren't working and more intense help from an outside resource may be necessary.

In short, referral to a qualified professional ought to be made when a teenager's behavior begins to interfere with his or her ability to carry out daily routines or sustain relationships (Les Parrott III, *Helping the Struggling Adolescent*).

ideas

Sample Youth Meeting
—Anger

OPENING DISCUSSION

- What kinds of things make you most angry?
- How do you tend to act when you get angry?
- Do you think it's a sin to get angry? Why or why not?
- Is anger ever right? If so, when?
- Did Jesus ever get angry? If so, when? How did he handle his anger?
- Can you think of any constructive ways to handle anger?

ATTENTION GRABBER

In this activity, you'll inflate three balloons to illustrate ways of handling anger. After blowing up the first one, let it go so it careens wildly around the room. Then explain how unpredictable and destructive uncontrolled anger can be. Blow up the second one until it pops, illustrating how anger that is denied or unexpressed eventually explodes. Then blow up the third one, but let out the air in a controlled way in front of a pinwheel, making the pinwheel go around. Explain how anger, when it is recognized and harnessed, can lead to constructive action.

SCRIPTURE STUDY

- The Bible says a lot about anger. Discuss each of these passages.
    Proverbs 15:1
    Proverbs 29:11
    James 1:19
    Ephesians 4:26
- What are some ways God has helped you with your anger?

WRAP-UP

Anger is a normal emotion that may come from feeling frustrated, disappointed, alienated, or hurt. While we can't control how we feel, we can control how we respond to our feelings. Some of us just fly off the handle like the wild balloon. Others of us tend to stuff anger until we eventually explode. But when we face our anger, asking God to help us deal with it constructively, good can actually come as a result of it.

a place to belong
Connecting With Gifted and Talented Youth

TONY TAMBERINO • Associate for Youth and Young Adult Ministry • St. John the Evangelist Church • Columbia, Maryland

A s I spoke with Terry, a dad with three kids in our youth program, he shared some thoughts on his work as a teacher with gifted and talented (GT) students. Terry told me his starting point in working with such young people is to tell them, "It's not a question of how smart you are, but how you are smart!" That conversation, nearly four years ago, has had a real impact on my work with young people.

In recent years the expansion of such gifted and talented programs has touched almost every school. Schools recognize that each young person is unique. Students learn and develop at different rates, and different educational approaches are necessary if every student is to reach his or her potential. These programs certainly include young people who traditionally would be placed in an advanced track, young people with high general intelligence or with high aptitude in traditional academic areas (such as mathematics, science, and verbal skills). But there also has been a proliferation of GT curricula focus on specific skill areas, such as computer skills, business, fine arts (particularly music and drama), and athletics. (For information on multiple intelligences, see www.familyeducation.com/article/0,1120,4-6245,00.html.) In addition, the increasing competition for college entrance and scholarships puts tremendous pressure on young people to focus their lives and concentrate much of their time, energy, and talent on very specific areas.

Many of these GT young people seem to have busier lives than your average youth worker, who has trouble remembering her or his home decor. Some of these young people want to be involved in everything and have difficulty prioritizing; others take so narrow a focus that it seems their lives are only about drama or computers or soccer or obtaining college money.

While gifted and talented programming is a wonderful educational development, it helps create an attitude among many young people that presents some definite challenges for youth ministry. Many gifted and talented youth struggle with

- an overemphasis on grades and a high grade point average;
- healthy self-respect and self-worth ("Am I valuable only because I'm good at something?");
- four or five hours of homework, on average, per night;
- the pressure to have a résumé that reads as if they have ten years of work experience;
- a lack of social opportunities that connect them to a group that welcomes and accepts them regardless of their ability to produce; and
- fear of trying new things in the face of sticking with the familiar and comfortable.

Connecting such GT kids to youth ministry programs can seem a daunting task. Like the young man in Mark 10 who asked Jesus, "What must I do to inherit eternal life?", our gifted and talented youth are seeking to belong, are searching for meaning. How do we make contact? Can we break through time constraints and overly scheduled lives? What can we offer to attract these young people's interest, particularly when compared with what is offered at school or in community programs?

- Develop a church Web page since many young people in general and GT youth in particular are really into computers and browsing the Internet. Include pictures of activities, a general invitation to participate in a youth group that welcomes everyone, a schedule of upcoming events, and the youth office phone number. Ask some youth group members, with adult supervision, to compose the Web page. If possible, establish a church chat room so young people can make contact with peers who have similar interests. Be sure to include articles and features written by the young people themselves and personal profiles of members of the group. Publish the Web address in all church publications, bulletin boards, and mailings. Include it in the church letterhead. Also provide each member of your group with fliers introducing the Web page to be handed out at school and other activities.

- Send out monthly youth newsletters that include reviews of local school plays, recitals, and activities—not just youth group news. GT kids who are often heavily involved in these kinds of activities may be attracted to a group that takes an interest in outside activities.

- Attend local math and science fairs, school plays, recitals, concerts, and athletic events. Gifted and talented young people are often strongly represented at such events. This shows interest and allows for personal contact with other young people who don't come to church or youth ministry activities. Perhaps a youth worker could attend with a small group of kids from that particular school. Adult members of the youth ministry committee also should be recruited to attend school events and provide a presence, since it's impossible for one or two youth workers to attend every school function and event.

- Compose brief articles for the neighborhood paper or local high school roundup, if available. Offer a special invitation to kids with special interests or hobbies. For example, an invitation to musicians might catch the attention of young people who spend much of their time practicing instruments. Mention the possibility of becoming part of the church music ministry or even the youth music ministry. Publicize a calendar of events and highlight accomplishments and projects of the youth group. Always include phone numbers and e-mail addresses for contact.

- Take out ads in local high school literary magazines, theater programs, sports banquet programs, and yearbooks. Include your logo, a contact person, and the youth ministry office phone number and e-mail address.

- Organize an outreach team of young people who are charged with inviting their friends and acquaintances from school and community programs (such as the computer club, drama and art classes, and the travel soccer team). This outreach team should be instructed to "target" individual young people who aren't connected to a youth group or church. The team could create a button or a sticker to hand out at various events and gatherings. It could say something like "Come and see!" or "Looking for a place to belong?" and the name of the group.

- Recruit a team of parents and other caring adults who will communicate regularly through notes, e-mail, or phone calls to one or two GT kids in your church. Some gifted and talented young people have difficulty connecting with peers, but do rather well with adults. Caring adults who foster nurturing relationships with such young people can be a conduit for helping them connect with others in the group.

Have members of this adult care team write initial notes on behalf of the youth ministry, inviting them to participate. These notes should mention the following:

  - that their presence is important at youth activities and events,
  - that they're special and their gifts and talents are needed (be as personal as possible, mentioning specific gifts and talents),
  - that the youth ministry offers an opportunity to belong to a group that both values and respects each individual,
  - that there are people who care about them and are there for support and encouragement, and
  - that they're invited to attend any youth ministry event.

- Lead a Bible study on 1 Corinthians 12:3-11. Invite each person to bring a shoe box for decorating. Provide wrapping paper, glue, crayons and markers, paints, magazines, and other art supplies so each person can create a gift box that symbolizes his or her talents. After the boxes are decorated, allow some time for everyone to view all the gift boxes. Then allow each person to explain his or her decorations.

- Offer special opportunities for church and community service. Have the group share in local or state Special Olympics as coaches, officials, and buddies. Participate in a local CROP Walk with young people asking the church community for pledges. Arrange a cystic fibrosis fund-raising event, such as karaoke night, a basketball marathon, a bowling tournament, or a car wash. Ask each member to bring a friend, preferably one who isn't connected to youth ministry. Many GT kids find service opportunities very attractive. In addition to offering a break from routine, they present the chance to give of themselves and help others. Helping young people focus on others' needs is a valuable developmental asset, especially since many GT young people spend so much time with others like themselves. (For more information on developmental assets, refer to *Healthy Communities, Healthy Youth*, Search Institute, Minneapolis, MN, 1993. www.search-institute.org.)

- Lead a Bible study on 1 Corinthians 12:12-30. Offer a lesson that highlights the diversity of each individual and how important differences are in the whole church. Help the young people articulate how different gifts can work together toward a common goal. Follow this Bible study with an activity that utilizes the different gifts of the group for a common result. For example, plan and prepare a meal for residents of a local retirement home, organize a food collection for a local pantry, or prepare a social gathering for the younger children of the church.

- Develop a peer ministry team that empowers young people to serve as peer helpers and companions in church ministry to other youth. A peer ministry team should receive training in understanding the Bible, the person of Jesus Christ, discipleship, small-group facilitation, peer-responding skills, and conflict resolution. Peer ministers could serve as small-group facilitators and assistants for Christian education classes, youth retreats, confirmation study groups, and middle school events. Peer ministers also can share their faith stories at worship services and other activities. Such ministry opportunities highlight gifts and talents not ordinarily used by young people.

- Conduct an annual youth retreat on the theme "Who Am I and Where Am I Going?" Market the experience as a chance for youth to get away and discover more about themselves and others. Incorporate plenty of time for journaling and guided reflection. Also include in the activities an instrument like "The Keirsey Temperament Sorter" (David Keirsey and Marilyn Bates, *Please Understand Me*) with a presentation on understanding the meaning and value of such a profile. Discuss what each person can contribute to the body of Christ.

- Lead a Bible study on the parable of the talents, Matthew 25:14-30. Have young people form small groups, and ask each group to develop a modern adaptation of the parable in skit form. Ask them to be creative, using music, props, humor, and other fun elements. Require that each person take part in the performance. After all the skits have been performed, lead a discussion about why people bury their talents and gifts and how we can encourage others to share them. End the session with an opportunity for each person to name a gift they recognize in someone else. Conclude by playing "Treasure of You" by Steven Curtis Chapman from *Heaven in the Real World*.

- Establish an elder-care team to lead a bimonthly or monthly worship service for residents at a local nursing home. Some young people have a wonderful way with the elderly, and such contact between young people and the elderly can be extremely beneficial for both groups. For GT kids, such contact helps them to focus on people skills and Christian humility. Offer some preliminary training on the aging process, Alzheimer's disease, and working with the elderly. (Note: It's best to bring in trained professionals for this training, since they'll be better able to answer any questions young people might have.) The worship service might include these elements:

- some simple hymns in sing-along style,
- Scripture readings,
- a brief reflection on Scripture,
- some intercessory prayer concluding with the Lord's Prayer,
- a blessing, and
- a closing hymn.

Conclude the visit with a light snack and some time for personal visiting.

● Develop and train a children's worship team of high school and middle school youth. Recruit the youth to work with children during Sunday worship, leading Scripture teaching, crafts, and other activities that help the children apply God's Word to their lives. Some young people who might not be comfortable in a peer setting might be well-suited for this kind of activity. In the same vein, some youth could be recruited for baby-sitting services in the Sunday nursery.

● Provide opportunities for young people to be involved in local community service projects that highlight skills they usually don't use in school. Working with Habitat for Humanity, the Christian Appalachian Project, or Christmas in April can draw gifted and talented young people into working with their hands or with tools. Many of these organizations seek to partner with church and youth ministry groups.

● Devote a youth group meeting to game night. Invite young people to bring and play their favorite board and computer games. Gifted and talented kids love to play games—board games and computer games in particular. Game nights offered on an occasional basis could become a hook to draw GT kids into the larger group.

● Organize a Coffeehouse where young people can showcase their talent. Invite groups to audition to perform music and song, poetry readings, stand-up comedy, juggling, mime, and other entertainment. Serve coffee and soft drinks, and create an atmosphere of comfort and hospitality. Advertise on school and community bulletin boards, at the public library, and in the church bulletin and Web page. Also host one youth meeting a year for Open-Mike Night. Be sure to screen acts to avoid anything inappropriate, but keep this informal so untried talent can have an opportunity to "get their feet wet."

● Arrange a fine arts and gallery night. Invite student artists to display their drawings, paintings, sketches, sculptures, pottery, and other artwork. Have someone from a local art museum offer a brief presentation on opportunities for artists in the area. Be sure to send fliers and announcements to the art departments in local high schools.

● Send notes of congratulations to local young people who win scholarships, athletic titles, and other accolades. Send an opening-night telegram or note (if telegrams are too expensive) to the cast of the high school play. Make sure the youth ministry newsletter also includes an accolade page that highlights the most recent accomplishments of group members and those who have made the honor roll at their schools.

● Recruit a team of young people to act as photographers and videographers at all youth events and activities. This idea will be particularly attractive to young people with a special interest and talent for photography and movie-making as well as artistic types who love to create and display collages, bulletin boards, and posters. The finished products could then be used as publicity and marketing tools that highlight the diversity of interests and talents among the youth of the church. Display pictures and show videos of particular events during social time after worship, at Christian education programs, and in the entrance area of the church. Make a documentary video of youth talking about their experiences as participants in the youth activities of the church. The message that youth ministry respects and welcomes everyone's gifts and talents will come through loud and clear.

● Send a letter of introduction to every middle school and high school principal in your area, offering support and help any time they might feel the need to contact you. Provide a list of your activities and events along with a yearly calendar. Ask them for a copy of their calendar in return. Be sure to note any particular skills you may have (you're a licensed counselor, you offer crisis intervention, you provide tutoring, and so on). Such contact with the schools lets people in the community know your group is welcoming and offers a host of activities and events that will appeal to a large segment of the youth population. School administrators, teachers, and parents will have one more source to which they can refer—especially when faced with a GT young person who doesn't seem to be connected to a group that both welcomes and affirms him or her.

CHAPTER

11

weaving a new fabric

Ministering to Young People in Blended Families

ROBERT KLIMEK • Liturgy and Music Director • Our Lady of Fatima Church • Lakewood, Colorado

A solitary tree grew on a little-traveled road. In the summer it offered shade and fresh pears to all who passed. One spring, as the tree began to bud and bear fruit, a Doubt crept up and spoke into its ear: "Is a pear the best you have to offer?"

Immediately, an Idea spoke an answer into the tree's other ear. "Apples might be better," it said, "for they could easily be stored in pockets during a long journey." Quickly, the tree began to grow apples where pears once had been.

Early on the next day, a second Doubt whispered to the tree, "Won't apples be too hard and too common?"

Quickly, the Idea returned and made a reply to the tree, "You should grow plums, for they are soft and most special, not common at all! That night, delicate plums filled all the spots where once there had been pears and then apples.

On the third day, it rained. When the showers stopped the tree glanced at its reflection in a nearby puddle. On every branch hung fruit that was part green pear, part red apple, and part purple plum. People began to avoid the tree, for they feared its fruit had somehow become poisonous.

After several days of loneliness, the tree decided to rid itself of the exotic, multicolored fruit. Immediately it began to bear a crop of new spring pears. Soon visitors returned to visit the tree and to sample its sweet offering.

In our culture, blended families are becoming more and more visible. They aren't a new phenomenon, though. They've always been there: grandchildren living with their grandparents, a teenager moving in with an unrelated family, two single-parent families joined together by a marriage. But a reality shift occurred with the advent of the electronic age. This medium made it possible for us to see the goings-on of other family types, not over the back fence, but over the air waves. TV and films revealed the lifestyles of others and made them more visible. This exposure has widened the definition of family in our culture.

In the entertainment industry, it has become the norm to showcase a variety of family situations. Film companies like Disney have frequently highlighted a blended-family model. *The Parent Trap* is about twins and their divorced parents. Dumbo, since he was a stork delivery, has no father and is raised by a circus mouse and a female elephant group. Pinocchio is adopted by a single elderly father and a cricket.

Family life is a set of living relationships. Divorce and separation make for "dead," or better still, "nonliving," relationships. Growth is no longer available between people experiencing this type of relationship termination. Divorce is like a dead spot on the front lawn of an expensive mansion. Everyone can see that the spot is dry and lifeless, but no one is allowed to mend it. All types of lawn ornaments can be placed on or around it, but these only mask the situation. The spot remains. Members of mixed or blended families live in such a situation. The teenagers involved are pulled between the nonliving feelings of the past and the new growth of the present.

Teenagers involved in mixed families experience a "death and dying" process. They must move from what used to be before they can resurrect into what is and can be. Like the pear tree, these young people have to accept the fact that their new family situation will bear a new and different, but living, fruit. As in the case of the tree, these teenagers need to go through a period of change and adaptation before settling back into...themselves.

Occasionally childish or bullish, then totally compliant at other times, young people can exhibit a variety of characteristics in front of their parent figures. All this behavior serves to help bring the new guardians up-to-date on who the teenagers are and how they arrived at this "who." Teenagers may even attempt to relive earlier parts of their lives that may have been missed when ties in their original family began to fray.

So as you work with teenagers in blended families, it's important to remember these four points:

■ Blended families are not new to our culture.

■ Certain types of blended families (divorced) can have a dead spot in relationships.

■ Teenagers in blended families must experiment and then settle into being in a new growing family environment.

■ Teenagers in blended families experience hard but workable moments throughout the year.

- It's important to realize that family blending occurs whenever two or more dissimilar histories (personal stories) are combined. Biological families get a chance to slowly grow a family life. Blended teenagers come with a prepackaged history and have to learn, accept, and eventually promote a new life story.

- Meditate on Matthew 1:18-25. Joseph, at this moment in his life, was realizing his own blended-family situation.

- When inquiring about a blended teenager's background, always start with an open-ended question. Get the teenager to talk about his or her family experience in general terms. Ask about vacations, customs, or something similar. Give examples from your own background.

- Don't assume that blended-family children are "troubled." They definitely have issues to deal with, but these many not be any more difficult than those of a "traditional" family experience.

- Consider holding a "Heritage Meeting." Make this a time where teenagers have a chance to show off skills handed down to them by parents, grandparents, friends, and others. Hold a preparatory meeting to help the group develop a way to search for these gifts.

- Encourage family participation in your group. Hold family nights. Each time, have a different host family introduce the youth to some of their customs and traditions.

- Model your own background. Everyone has areas in their past that are unlike a traditional family background. Talk openly about these unique characteristics.

- Seek out a responsible adult with blended-family experience, and ask him or her to be an integral resource to your youth program.

- Either directly or indirectly, structure your youth group to resemble a family. Talk about the different roles in a strong family. Spot these roles in your youth group. Note: The youth group itself is not a traditional family unit, yet it can act and grow as one. Ask your teenagers a variety of questions about your youth group family. Who will take care of finances? Why? Who makes major decisions? Why? Who cleans up? Why?

- Get together with other youth groups and have a "blended-family" night. Use a *Bible Mystery Event* (Group Publishing) as an icebreaker.

- Contact all organizations that can inform your group about people who live and operate effectively in nontraditional family settings. Have them speak to your teenagers. Here are some suggestions:

  - foster parents,
  - foreign and domestic adoption agencies,
  - divorced parents groups, or
  - juvenile parole officers.

- Match up "blended" kids. Instead of meeting over a cup of coffee, supply them with burgers or pizza and let them "talk it out" in the youth room.

- Realize that it's normal for members of blended families to feel like they're between two opposing forces. Many times, the teenagers don't perceive a clear line of communication between separated marriage partners. This inconsistency gives a teenager the feeling of having no clear-cut boundaries.

- Communicate regularly with the adults immediately responsible for these special teenagers. Don't find yourself in the position of being a go-between for warring parents.

- If a teenager is having problems with a mixed family, encourage that person to air these feelings with his or her caregivers. If the issue is too hot to handle comfortably, suggest the use of a third party listener. A listener is someone both the parents and the teenager can trust. If a family doesn't have a person to fill this role, suggest a list of confidential listeners with whom you're familiar. As a youth worker, don't compromise your position by taking on the role of the official listener.

- Teenagers in blended families must know where to go when things happen. They have to clearly perceive who's in charge and who's calling the shots. Suggest this as a beginning topic for a "listener" session. Also, keep your lines of communication clear with them.

- Blended teenagers need a healthy idea of relationship. If this isn't present between the birth parents, it will be difficult for the teenagers to understand. Find a tape of an old TV show or movie dealing with family. Give this to a group of teenagers. Have the group study a section of the video and re-create it at a youth meeting, costumes and all. Discuss what's really being said behind the acting and the lines. Where is respect shown? How is trust displayed? Where is the unreality in this story? Where is the reality? Then, find a current TV show or movie involving a nontraditional family. Again, have a group re-create a scene from it. Repeat the discussion.

- Understand that people in blended families are frequently caught in time conflicts. Their schedules are often upset and redirected. In a traditional family, plans get changed. In blended families, several sets of changeable plans are involved. The teenager may get involved with youth group one week and be absent the next because of a second parent's schedule. These youth often feel embarrassed if it's impossible for them to make a commitment to anything because they don't get a chance to settle in one location. Consistency is totally lacking in their lives.

- Adapt your schedule so blended teenagers can be a critical part of your youth program, even when away. Assign them tasks they can accomplish between meetings or through e-mail.

● Regularly use e-mail, postcards, and phone calls to keep everyone up-to-date on the activities in your group.

● Make sure blended teenagers' names are on all address lists, get-well cards, and on anything else relating to the youth group.

● Recognize that blended teenagers can be caught in a "wishing" mode. This can skew their perspective on their current situation. The time before they were part of this mixed situation can appear to be, with time and distance, a gentler, happier one. The demanding present isn't as comforting as the hazy past. Add to this the fact that half-siblings and second parents have been typically cast as the "evil" stepsister or mother, and these stereotypes become hard to see through.

● Strive to convey the thought that blended-family situations are not easy, in fact they can be tough, but they're very doable.

● Remember that holidays (especially Mother's Day, Father's Day, vacation time, Thanksgiving, and Christmas) can be challenging. Teenagers can find themselves unable to explain their unique families to others from a more traditional background. Be present for them as they go through the experience of giving up past memories and adopting new ones.

● Be ready to recommend resources or have them available for "home delivery" or "take out." A vast amount of fictional child and young adult literature is available on the topic of blended families. Most of it presents blended families as interesting and exciting. Seek out and learn some of these stories by heart.

● Do some spontaneous theater. Have kids create and act out one-minute stories based on how it would feel to

- be adopted,
- be a foster child,
- be from another country,
- speak a different language,
- have different family customs,
- no longer be an only child, or
- divorce or separate from someone.

● Make sure parents in blended families are aware of all support groups available to them. Do some footwork and gather a list. Arrange the list in order of the degree of commitment necessary.

● In cases where a family and/or a teenager is in need of counseling, ask yourself these questions:

- Does your church have a sufficient amount of money set aside for counseling services?
- Can you start your own support group and bring in speakers?

playing by the rules

Building Relationships With Student Athletes

Bo Boshers • Executive Director of Student Ministries •
Willow Creek Association • South Barrington, Illinois

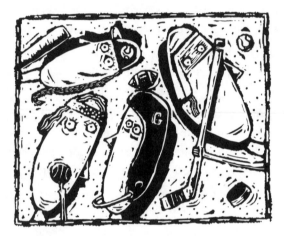

Y ou probably have several students in your ministry who are athletes participating on sports teams at their schools and clubs in the community. Student athletes have many strengths to offer your ministry. First, athletes demonstrate high levels of commitment and discipline in order to compete. They work hard to improve their skills through regular training. This athletic discipline can apply to spiritual life. Because they know what it takes to improve athletically, many student athletes can more easily understand the concept of spiritual disciplines and take steps to grow in their personal relationships with God.

Also, student athletes are used to being motivated by coaches and teammates, and they understand the importance of short-term goals.

They like to be challenged and want to know the truth. These traits can be used in kingdom work as well. A student athlete will most likely embrace a challenge toward personal spiritual growth or evangelism. Student athletes will accept challenges and strive to see positive results.

Student athletes understand teamwork and may have strong relational skills. Sports give many students confidence, and they may not be afraid to take a stand for Christ with their peers. They understand the team concept and what it feels like to belong to something. They may have compassion for their non-Christian friends, especially those who don't belong to anything. Student athletes may be the ones to invite friends to ministry events and help build a sense of team and community within your ministry. With the right training in evangelism, student athletes can make a big difference for Christ on their campuses and sports teams.

In addition, student athletes have great opportunities to be a testimony to those around them because they're often in the spotlight on their campuses. How they win and lose and conduct themselves both on and off the playing field provides chances to model Christlike character. You can challenge and encourage them to be positive examples. They also can reflect Christ in the way they treat sports rivals from other schools—Christian athletes can be highly competitive yet still treat their rivals with respect, fairness, and good sportsmanship.

Not only is it important to know the strengths of student athletes, it's also necessary to look at the potential obstacles you may face in reaching out to this particular group of students. One of those obstacles is that student athletes are busy. During sports seasons, practices and games occupy much of their free time. You may need to meet with them one-on-one at different times or make exceptions that allow their small groups to meet at more convenient times. Sundays may be the best day to connect with student athletes, either one-on-one or at ministry programs.

Building a relational bridge with the student athlete may look different during sports seasons and may take more time. Due to evening games, many will miss your ministry programs and events. Even though they learn to balance a lot—homework, sports, and family— additional activities like church are often cut from the schedule. Be sensitive to their schedules, and be patient. The season will end. Remember that they're fulfilling important commitments they've made, just as you teach them about the importance of being committed to a relationship with Christ.

Another obstacle is that sometimes the students' identities become their sports. They become known on the campus for their talents instead of who they really are. Their confidence can soar with every victory and sag with each defeat. They can feel tremendous pressure to perform and win (either self-inflicted or from parents or coaches). As a youth worker, don't get caught in this trap. Minister to individuals for who they are, not for what they do.

Yet another potential obstacle is the issue of self-esteem. Winning athletes may struggle with arrogance, while athletes who lose or sit on the bench all season may have feelings of low self-esteem. If student athletes can grasp and understand the concept of their true identity in Christ, it will free them up to reach their full potential as athletes. More important, it will help them grow in their relationship with God.

On the following pages, you'll find numerous ideas to help you more effectively reach out to student athletes and build relationships with them.

SMALL GROUPS

Small groups are an excellent way to maximize life change and to build relationships among students. A small group of students can experience authentic community by loving one another, encouraging one another, praying for one another, teaching one another, and accepting one another.

● Use small groups to teach about topics relevant to athletes and to give them a chance to discuss and learn from peers who have similar interests. Possible topics might include building character, being an example, pressure and performance, winning for Christ, perseverance, motivation, cheating and swearing, power under control, dealing with anger, self-image, and how to compete on and off the field.

● Create devotionals specifically targeted to individual athletes or a small group of athletes, and give them to the athletes during their sports season. Great verses to use are Jeremiah 29:11; Ephesians 5:1-2; Philippians 3:12-14; 4:13; Colossians 3:17; Hebrews 10:23-24; 12:1-3.

● Identity in Christ is an important issue for athletes. Too often a student's identity gets wrapped up in his or her sport and confusion sets in concerning who they are vs. what they do. They need teaching on who they are in Christ, and they need to understand that Christ is the foundation of their lives. This topic would be a great study for a small group of student athletes.

● Another powerful study for a small group of student athletes is a look at the qualities of Jesus as they relate to athletics. Jesus was always under control. He faced numerous obstacles, yet he never quit. He treated everyone with respect. Encourage small groups to study New Testament passages that highlight who Jesus is.

SPIRITUAL GROWTH

Helping students grow spiritually is an awesome responsibility and one that shouldn't be taken lightly. As you provide practical and applicable spiritual teaching for students, they'll learn how God can play an active role, both on and off the field, in their daily lives.

● All sports have lines to indicate boundaries for the playing field or court. When you're "between the lines" (BTL), it means you're a player. Athletes want to be players and know that they need to stay "between the lines" and not run out of bounds and risk disqualification. This concept can be used to teach students about staying "between the lines" spiritually and how to stay in a right relationship with God. Print the phrase "Stay BTL" on locker stickers or key chains as a spiritual challenge for students. You might even consider starting a "BTL" club for student athletes, meeting with them before school or on Sundays.

● Challenge students to choose a season verse and memorize it. They might want to post it in their lockers or write it on their gym shoes as a reminder.

● Teach athletes about the importance of playing for an audience of One rather than the applause of the crowd. Remind them that Christ is more concerned with the development of their character than the scoreboard. This will free them up to perform to the best of their abilities instead of feeling pressure.

● Challenge students to live for God and play their sports at "212." Water boils at 212 degrees—this means it's hot, not lukewarm. As Christians, all of us should be "hot" and not fall into a complacent (lukewarm) relationship with God. This also applies to athletics. God has gifted some students athletically, and they should be challenged to go all out and do their best, not give half-efforts or be lazy. Provide visual reminders of this concept: door hangers with "212" printed on them for students' bedrooms or note cards they can tape to the bathroom mirror.

EVANGELISM

Student athletes most likely have already built relationships with non-Christians on their sports teams. Encourage them to pray for their teammates during their season. Take time throughout the ministry season to train student athletes in effective ways to reach these friends.

● Invite a guest speaker, like a professional athlete or coach, to talk to your group of student athletes. Encourage your Christian students to bring friends, like non-Christian teammates, and use the event as outreach. Organizations like Fellowship of Christian Athletes (FCA), (800) 289-0909, and Athletes in Action, (877) 924-7478, are great resources for speakers.

● Organize sports tournaments for your Christian students to invite their non-Christian teammates and friends from school. To challenge the Christian students, tell them they can participate in a tournament only if they bring non-Christian friends. Try to coordinate sporting events according to the seasons they're played. For example, around Thanksgiving time during football season, hold a Turkey Bowl (a flag football tournament for guys and girls). Or during March Madness, organize a basketball tournament for guys and girls. Be sure to plan these tournaments with excellence—hire referees, order tournament T-shirts, make a draw sheet and post it, and so on. Athletes love to be competitive, and they are used to organized and well-run events. To cover costs, charge a fee for all participants. Sports tournaments help build ministry momentum, and excitement levels are high.

● Use sports as a way to connect with athletes who visit your ministry. Try to keep current on local and professional sports so you have an easy way to start conversations. Be prepared and know ways to engage student athletes and the friends they bring to ministry programs.

PROGRAMS

Developing programs that will reach the student athletes and relate to their world requires creativity and careful planning.

● Offer some healthy competition at your programs to allow relationships to be built and give many students a chance to participate. Athletes especially enjoy competition, and using this element in your program may help break down walls students have put up toward church. A great resource for competition ideas is *Impact Sports: Creative Competitions for Team Building* by Bo Boshers and Troy Murphy, published by Zondervan Publishing House.

You can also organize special theme competition nights. For example, offer a cheerleading contest with cheerleaders representing all the schools in your ministry. Or sponsor a slam-dunk competition featuring a few of the best basketball players in the area. A weightlifting competition may attract guys and girls who like to lift weights. Using different kinds of competition will draw a variety of students to your ministry.

● Organize events throughout the ministry season that will attract athletes. Use your particular location and environment to your advantage. Go rafting if you live close to a river. Play paintball. Play tug of war on the beach. Take your group skiing, ice-skating, or sledding. Go bowling or roller-skating. Do a sports night targeted to athletes and rotate stations between bowling, swimming, basketball, and football.

● Tie into your program themes that connect with what's happening in the world of sports. Think about the seasons. When the Olympics, the Super Bowl, the Stanley Cup playoffs, Wimbledon, The Masters, or March Madness are taking place, use them in your teaching time and small groups.

● Invite a professional athlete or coach to be a guest speaker at one of your programs.

● If possible, shoot video of local high school games in which students from your ministry are competing. Show video highlights at the next meeting. Or rent and show clips of a sports video that ties into the season.

RESOURCES

Take time to build a resource file of catalogs, books, and videos, as well as a list of people with whom you can network for additional ideas.

● Athletes regularly write autobiographies that might challenge and encourage the Christian athletes in your ministry. Keep current on what's available by visiting a local Christian bookstore.

● Let students know about Sports Spectrum, a great magazine for Christian athletes. It can be ordered by calling (800) 283-8333.

● Various Christian sports camps provide opportunities for athletes to build their skills. Two recommended camps are Kanakuk Kamp—located in Branson, Missouri—(417) 334-2432, and Fellowship of Christian Athletes (FCA) camps—offered around the country—(800) 289-0909.

● Before the Super Bowl in January, a video is released with interviews of several Christian NFL players. Use this video at a Super Bowl outreach event by showing the video before the game or at halftime. The video is produced by Athletes in Action, Lebanon, PA. Call (513) 933-2421 for more information.

● Use the Internet as a resource for sports-related information and ideas for games. Check student ministry organizations' Web sites, like www.group-publishing.com or www.YouthSpecialties.com, for new product information.

RELATIONSHIP-BUILDING

It can be challenging to build relationships with so many different students, but hopefully these ideas will help you as you strive to reach and lead this generation for Christ.

● Attend sporting events at the schools in your area. It's always helpful to see and experience the environment of the students you're reaching out to and to show an interest in their world. There always seems to be a big game or event to attend throughout the ministry season.

● Acquire the schedules of all sporting events from the local schools represented in your ministry. Post them on the church youth bulletin board and encourage your leaders to attend events whenever possible.

● Identify Christian coaches at area schools and build relationships with them. Offer to volunteer, if possible, at events throughout the year.

● If you have knowledge or expertise in a certain sport, investigate any coaching opportunities, whether volunteer or part time, at local schools. This might be a great way to build trust and credibility with students, especially athletes.

● Gather all the student athletes in your ministry for a meeting. Ask them to fill out cards indicating in which sports they participate and what their weekly schedules are like during the season. Give these cards to the appropriate small-group leaders and train them in how to reach out to these students.

- Be aware of how your student athletes are doing in their sports. Call them before big games and let them know you're praying for them. Follow up after the games and ask them how they did. Be sensitive to whether they've won or lost. If they've lost, take the opportunity to remind them that they're winners in Christ. Read the local paper for sports stories. Post any pictures or articles about your students on the church bulletin board.

- Write encouraging notes to your athlete students during their seasons. Be their cheerleader!

open arms
Ministering to New Students in School

DAN JESSUP · Regional Director · Young Life · Colorado Springs, Colorado

t's a big, new school, full of two thousand kids. Two thousand strange, unfriendly, somehow frightening kids, and you seem to be the only new kid in the whole world. You're new to town, so you don't know anything about anything—how to dress right, what slang to use, who's cool, who to avoid, what's in and what's out. It's so easy to make a mistake that will haunt you forever, and so hard to know how to do the right thing.

Maybe you've been there—maybe you know what the new kids face.

Kids can be cruel, sadly enough, and a new student is different and unknown—an easy target for cruelty.

Most kids have lots of friends already—to fit in a new one takes effort and interest, things many times in short supply in the adolescent heart. A new student doesn't know how to fit in, doesn't know the culture, the cues, all the subtle things that make up the mysterious chemistry of what a kid needs most—to belong. There is nothing more important to most kids than belonging, and a large part of belonging means not standing out or being different from everybody else.

What do kids do to adjust? Many times they make friends with the first people who come along and act friendly—and many times those people are exactly the wrong people to befriend. They can be loners, outcasts, oddballs, or troublemakers, and a new student can be marginalized or dragged into trouble without ever realizing it's happening. Often the easiest way to be accepted is to do dumb things.

This can also happen with a group that readily accepts a new person—needy, at-risk kids can band together, looking for what might be termed as co-conspirators. New kids, eager to be accepted and to have friends, can slide into the wrong group and into dangerous behavior completely unprecedented in their lives. The drinking/partying/drug using groups are simple to join because one's character or potential for friendship are not the litmus tests for entry into the group; participating in the risky activity are the dues to be paid.

Absent these negative opportunities, new kids can quickly become lonely and depressed. Grades can plummet, behavior at home can deteriorate along with previously happy family relationships, and hobbies they once enjoyed can either be abandoned or become obsessions. A peaceful family that was cheerfully planning a move in the previous setting can degenerate overnight into a stormy family wondering what on earth went wrong.

If the new student is from another country, either an immigrant or a repatriated citizen, then added to all of the above is culture shock, something often more profound (called "re-entry") for a returning citizen than for a foreigner. In such circumstances, a new student can retreat completely from the world, going straight from school to home to a lonely but unthreatening bedroom. Everything is unfamiliar territory, and when kids are cruel, the pain goes deep.

Whether we like it or not theologically, the most important thing on earth and in heaven for a kid is belonging, having friends, being accepted, ultimately being valued enough to feel loved, and it's a rare and probably disturbed kid who won't be willing to make significant sacrifices in order to be accepted.

All too often, we as youth workers become comfortable with the familiar kids who attend our group. We get complacent with the old kids and are less willing to take in the new. We can preach against cliques, but without knowing it, we ourselves can actually foster the attitude that creates cliques.

If we want to broaden our youth groups and reach out to new students, we must re-familiarize *ourselves* with what it's like to be new. You might do this by visiting another church (with an unfamiliar worship style) where nobody knows who you are and take note of the feelings, thoughts, and fears you have in the process. As useful would be to visit a new high school (after getting permission from school administrators)—the fear and discomfort you feel will mimic that felt by a new student in that same school. Walk through the halls between class periods, sit by yourself in the lunchroom, wish that you had worn something else, be forced to ask a stranger where the bathrooms are—if your reaction is simply "I don't belong here and everybody knows it," you have gained a valuable gut-level insight into the feelings of every new student in any school or church.

Our challenge as youth workers is to engage a young person in relationships that require reasonable and healthy sacrifices, relationships that ultimately are worth the sacrifices made because of the positive benefits of the friendships—love, acceptance, healthy role models, good self-image, and so on. If this can happen in the context of the faith—now, that's a good goal for a youth worker to have.

- Meet the new kids. That means finding out who they are and figuring out a way to meet them that is non-threatening and natural. A natural path to follow is through student leaders at the school. Student leaders can try several things:

  - Ask at the office for a list of new kids in each grade, who can then be contacted and invited to special outreach events, maybe one in their honor.
  - Volunteer to run a welcome program for new kids that extends beyond just the first week of school. It might even be possible for the wise youth worker to become an adult advisor/volunteer. The welcome program can include practical things like school and community orientation, but also should aim at helping the new kids get involved in healthy ways with kids in the school. (If such a program exists already in the school, then volunteering to help is a good option.)
  - Your student leaders might become mentors/buddies for the year with some of the new kids.

- Be creative in imagining the types of events a group for new kids might offer— interest/hobby questionnaires, tips from experts in moving and transition experiences, a special dinner before a school event which the group attends together, video/pizza nights, and so on. Youth workers are great at putting together fun events that will attract kids and keep them coming. Use your best stuff.

- New kids can get behind in their academics in a hurry. It's possible that they've come from a slightly different curriculum, or that their previous schools weren't as strong as the new school. It's also easy to be distracted by the stress of being alone and friendless in a new school and to neglect homework. Offer a short-term tutorial after school for new kids, using some of your student leaders. Provide drinks, free T-shirts, door prizes (from local merchants), and information about your own youth group activities.

- If your schools don't have a well-prepared orientation session for new students, volunteer to put one together during an assembly period or after school. Invite representatives from different school clubs (chess, foreign language, choir, drama, and so on) to make short presentations and to be available at tables with information sheets. Have your student leaders available to offer help and information as guides.

- If the schools will allow you to do so, put on a tour of the city using school buses. If using the buses isn't possible, use church vans, inviting different churches to participate. Hit all the spots where kids go—the malls, video arcades, movie theaters, fast-food spots, bowling alleys, whatever the kids in your town do for clean and legal fun. Once again, handing out freebies from local merchants (especially when you go inside several of their shops) would be super. Have your student leaders be tour guides, and encourage high humor. You might also note places in town to avoid for reasons of personal safety.

- Invite the parents of new kids to an orientation session. You can talk about the nature and character of the school and community, identifying the positive attributes and providing information about some of the inevitable negatives—problems with crime, drugs, gangs, alcohol, and so on. Family help services can also be presented, such as counseling centers and hospitals. People always want to know where the locals shop for good prices, where to get cars fixed by honest mechanics…let your own imagination and familiarity with your community help you here. Of course, mentioning your own ministry is perfectly legitimate in this context, especially after having talked about some of the dangers to kids in your town.

- The goal, remember, is twofold: to get your kids to make friends with the new kids, and to help the new kids integrate into the school. Don't have an evangelistic agenda. Talks about faith will flow naturally out of the relationships you build. So use your best creative stuff, but don't get the idea killed by the school board by compromising your integrity—be clear about the nature of any event you offer.

- If you don't get on this at the beginning of the year, the opportunity is gone. At best, it's a short-term program where relationships with individual kids might extend into a longer term. Still, new kids do move in during the year (an even harder time to arrive), and if your student leaders are heads-up, they'll keep an eye out for them.

- Multiply yourself; you can't do it all alone, nor is it wise to try. Focus on having kids you know—your Christian student leaders—befriend the new kids, and don't flood your activities with adults. Kids need friends their own ages. New kids have the same need, and you can provide them with potential friends who will be a positive influence in their lives. Your biggest challenge may be to get your own student leaders committed to the process. How might you do that?

  - Use Jesus' example by telling stories. The woman at the well was ostracized from her community, drawing her water in the evening when everybody else was home watching CNN. The lepers were social outcasts, condemned to solitary lives by ignorance, superstition, and fear.
  - Use biblical and other stories to tap into feelings and histories of your student leaders themselves. Talk about times in their lives when

they were new and didn't belong, about dumb things they've done or mistakes they've made, and risky behavior that they may have practiced when they entered a new situation. You probably have some student leaders who have moved around and will be eager to share their stories.

● You likely have kids in your youth group who are loners even within the youth group. What a great opportunity to challenge your leaders to look outside the cliques to those who don't belong and invite them in. In one of my groups, we had as one of our central philosophies of ministry the identification of marginalized kids. Our adult leaders would be directed at any event to look for kids who were lurking alone on the fringes, and to go over and talk to them. Even better would be to get your student leaders to be intentional about this. Some training sessions on how to start and continue conversations with strangers might be useful. Here are some good resources for questions:

■ *Would You Rather…?, Have You Ever…?, and What If…?,* published by Youth Specialties;
■ *The Book of Questions* and *The Kids' Book of Questions,* by Gregory Stock, Workman Publishing; and
■ *The Book of If,* Quality Paperback Book Club.

● As youth workers, we frequently overemphasize creative programming (we'll pay gold for a killer skit) at the expense of building relationships. A great program is wonderful for attracting kids, but what keeps them coming is an intentional effort to build relationships with them. This is especially true with kids new to your group. They can easily be entertained out in the real world. What they need from you is the chance to make a friend, to be listened to, responded to, and cherished. Jesus' model is not really that close to Steven Spielberg or Robin Williams; you model him better by cherishing kids. If you haven't developed a small-group, relationship-building aspect to your ministry, you're behind the curve. Here are some excellent resources:

■ *Building Community in Youth Groups* by Denny Rydberg, Group Publishing;
■ *Honest to God* by Bill Muir and Dave Bartlett, Fast Forward Publishing;
■ *Small-Group Body Builders* by Michael D. Warden, Group Publishing; and
■ *Up Close and Personal,* by Wayne Rice, Zondervan Publishers.

● Interview five foreign exchange students and ask them what it's been like to come to a new country and school. Find out what would have made the transition easier.

● Brainstorm with your current youth group about what a new person coming to your church community might feel, and how you together could make your ministry more welcoming to new students.

● Have a competition to see how many new students your youth group kids can meet in the first month of the school year. Develop a prayer list of names and then make an effort to get to know each one personally. Find out if they have church homes or denominations. Don't simply try to recruit to your church, but set for yourself a goal to help plug them into ministry environments that will work for them.

pointing to God's love

Ministering to Teenagers in Dating Relationships

D. Scott Miller • Associate Director • National Federation for Catholic Youth Ministry • Washington, D.C.

L ove can be very confusing, especially for young people. Their music and their movies are always making suggestions about love—how to conduct the pursuit for love, when it really is love, the joy and pain of love. Young people are searching for guidance regarding the ways of love. Churches that choose not to address issues of love, dating, and intimacy stand the risk of missing one of the acute needs of developing adolescents. The challenge for us to define love is further complicated by a common cultural definition that often equates love with physical intimacy. Here are some statistics (from the Spring 1999 edition of Certified Registered Nurse Practitioner):

POINTING TO
GOD'S LOVE

99

- Fifty-six percent of women and 73 percent of men have become sexually active before their eighteenth birthday.
- About 25 percent of sexually experienced teens become infected with a sexually transmitted disease/infection each year.
- One million teenagers become pregnant each year, resulting in 14 percent intended births, 37 percent unintended births, 35 percent abortions, and 14 percent miscarriages.

Young people need to hear the church's message in the same light that two disciples heard the challenge on the road to Emmaus (Luke 24:13-35). Like the disciples (24:17), today's youth have moments of heartbreak regarding love relationships. Breakup, jealousy, embarrassment, and regrets are all part of the learning and growing process of developing intimate relationships.

Not unlike the Emmaus-bound disciples, today's young people have enough information regarding intimacy and love to make them sick to their stomachs. The statistics listed above are often replayed for young people. If churches only address the heartbreak of young people, they miss the implications of the Emmaus walk. After listening to the disciples' tale, Jesus helped them make sense of their story. He made so much sense, the disciples concluded their day by describing their hearts as burning within them (24:32).

Effective ministry with young people in dating relationships is about encouraging young people to recognize that their own "heart-burning" experiences are mere hints of the love God has for them.

ATMOSPHERE

● Invite young people to share their faith with their friends by bringing them to church activities. There are not many places in the adolescent world that are perceived as "date-friendly." That list might include a movie theater, a school dance or sports activity, or a house left unsupervised by working or busy adults. Make sure your church and your church activities are added to that informal list of places that are teen-tested and teen-approved.

● Establish standards of behavior for couples at your events. Make it clear that these standards are developed out of respect for the other participants as well as ensuring that everyone will be able to participate fully and freely throughout the program. A common rule of thumb is "what would be acceptable at your grandparents' dinner table."

● Remind your student leaders that church youth programs are a safe, fun, and inexpensive way to have parent-approved double dates or group dates. They're also great ways to introduce new members to your group or church.

● Discourage teenagers from inappropriate public displays of affection. They also should be mindful not to monopolize one another's time or attention. When planning icebreakers or warm-up activities, endeavor to be sensitive to games that might near or cross someone's boundaries for physical space or emotional maneuvering. Games that model inappropriate flirting behaviors or questionable persuasion tactics should be avoided, even in the name of fun.

SKILL DEVELOPMENT

● Sponsor communication workshops. Be attentive to the differences in communication patterns between men and women. There are many popular secular and Christian materials that address healthy communication between men and women.

● Young people need a safe place to appropriately express and understand feelings. Do this in games or role-plays, providing neutral opportunities for trusted adults and peers to provide feedback and positive critique. This also allows participants opportunities to attempt to "read" the emotions of another.

● Manners and etiquette are still important, if not often taught or discussed, in today's world. A workshop that emphasizes simple etiquette might be valuable for the kids in your group. Emphasize showing respect for others, making eye contact, shaking hands, using silverware and napkins at a meal, and other standards of behavior. You might even build this around a lesson on prayer—approaching God with reverence, respect, and thanksgiving.

● For young people who are dating while active in your church activities, this question might come up: What's the right way or "Christian way" to break up? Young people need help in assessing the appropriateness of their dating choices. Chap Clark, in *Next Time I Fall in Love,* suggests that young people work on maintaining a sense of equal intimacy in emotions, time, physical touch, facts and feelings shared, and commitment.

PROGRAMMING

● Here's a discussion-starting point for a parent meeting regarding young people and dating. Ask parents to remember back to an early positive, significant, or meaningful experience of touch—holding hands, a kiss, walking arm-in-arm—while dating. In small groups, have them briefly answer the following questions:

■ If you had a time machine and could take a picture of the moment you're remembering, how would it look? (Describe the picture with only facts and details, no emotions.)
■ What are three feelings you had at that moment?
■ What was happening at the time?
■ What made that touch positive, significant, or meaningful?

If your group is like most, many faces will be warmed with happy memories. Tell the group you're moving on to the next activity. Ask the group to write a headline for your church newspaper. Headlines are very brief and succinct. The headline must be related to the church's message to teenagers about dating, love, and sex. Allow no discussion—just immediate brainstorms. There will probably be a noticeable mood change. Headlines might include "Don't Do It," "Save Sex," or "Wait."

Spend the remainder of the discussion talking about the incongruity between our own experiences and our message toward the next generation. Discuss appropriate ways to teach young people about love, sex, and dating.

● How can your church become involved in senior proms or other annual formal and socials? Hold church services before the event or the next day, and highlight teenagers' participation. Sponsor or cooperate with post-prom celebrations. Help organize group dates for many members, if appropriate, to the school's program. Develop alternatives for young people—perhaps a sit-down dinner without the expense of the formal clothing and the rest. Host alternative programming for younger students such a non-prom or a morp (prom spelled backward).

- Movies are full of stories of love and passion. Unfortunately, many young people only see love and passion in rated R or NC-17 scenes. What are examples of sacrificial love in the movies? Perhaps a movie discussion series would provide opportunities to expand the definitions of love and passion. It would be advisable to limit selections to the PG level. Mix in oldies and the classics with more familiar modern movies.

- World AIDS Day is celebrated on December 1 every year. Sponsor a prayer service for your community. It might be fitting to wear red ribbons during programming events or to do an educational program for young people and their families on this day.

- As an intergenerational event, invite parents to schedule dates with their young people for various programs. Schedule a father-daughter event or a mother-son event. Always make sure to have a backup list of trusted and safe adults to step in for young people who have family situations that might prevent their participation. A candlelight dinner or a weekend morning brunch, a speaker, a prayer service, or a combination of the above might be very appealing to families.

- Valentine's Day is another holiday for romantics. Fund-raisers that are designed to deliver Valentine's Day cards, singing telegrams, or sweets could be popular for the entire church community. While these efforts aren't meant to compete with culture, they do make a church activity seem relevant or even help redefine a culturally traditional activity.

- True Love Waits is an international campaign designed to challenge students to remain sexually abstinent until marriage. Hundreds of thousands of students have pledged, "Believing that true love waits, I make a commitment to God, myself, my family, my friends, my future mate, and my future children to be sexually abstinent from this day until the day I enter a biblical marriage relationship." Invite young people together for an extended evening discussing sexual decision-making and close with the commitment cards as part of a prayer service. Encourage young people with keepsakes of the event and by displaying their commitments in a public setting. For more information, see www.truelovewaits.com.

- As a faith community, take advantage of opportunities to celebrate commitments for sexual abstinence outside marriage. Young people need to see the model of single young adults who don't live a *Melrose Place* lifestyle and married couples who honor their commitments to one another.

AWARENESS

- Periodically remind participants that your activities are drug free/sober activities and that this is always the wisest choice for other nonchurch free time activities and dates.

- Many communities have a Crisis Pregnancy Center. Consider volunteer/service opportunities for your young people as well as fund-raising to support their efforts. These sites are often a source for speakers as well.

- Dating violence continues to be an often underaddressed issue for young people. Both males and females preparing to date should understand the "power and control" dynamics prevalent in violent relationships. Domestic-violence shelters as well as law-enforcement personnel might be helpful in this regard.

been there, done that, know that answer

Bringing Freshness to "Churched" Teenagers

KAREN DOCKREY • Youth Minister • First Baptist Church
Downtown • Nashville, Tennessee

eenagers who have grown up in the church have three main
struggles: challenge, confusion, and comfort.

"Churched" youth may find a severe lack of challenge at church.
They've already heard most Bible stories; they've already been
through umpteen group builders. The solution is to recognize that
these teenagers don't want to be ministered to as much as to be seen
as significant believers who make a real difference. They want to
know why and how to fulfill their unique purpose. They want to

delve deeply into agonizing questions of faith. They want to know how to apply real faith to the joys and sorrows of real life.

Churched teenagers also fight confusion. They may have asked faith questions that were swept under the rug with a "just believe." They don't understand why the people at church don't know, or won't tell, the answers to hard questions. They may have seen troubling happenings in the church. Perhaps a mean-spirited someone is respected and given power rather than the gentle servant who acts more like Jesus. Each time teenagers watch adults fail to value what God values, youth wonder if the Christian life is worth the hassle.

Finally, the comfort of churched teenagers can be a great asset or a hindrance. It's an asset when youth focus less attention on being part of the group, and more attention on learning and serving. But this can threaten some youth workers who want members to depend on them—the deep-seated security of churched kids works against some youth workers' I-can-fix-this-bunch-of-hurting-kids goal. Youth workers can move past this by deliberately affirming youth as members of the body of Christ. One youth may have a gift of mercy, one may have the gift of leadership, and still another, the gift of discernment. The gifts work together, not in competition with the worker's gift of administration (1 Corinthians 12). Healthy Christian teenagers depend on Jesus Christ as their head. The youth leader must encourage this, rather than point to himself or herself.

The comfort of churched teenagers is a hindrance when they neglect to reach out, grow cliquish, or forget how much others need a place to be at home with God and other people. Rather than nag them about this, show them what to do (see ideas on the following pages).

Be unafraid to approach church with churched teenagers. Let their comfort permeate the group. Deliberately coordinate their gift expression with each other and with other ages in the church to grow a healthy body of Christ. Wrestle tough questions with the confidence that we don't have to know all the answers to approach the Answer. Deliberately and specifically challenge each young person in your group to grow deeper, to overcome more permanently, and to serve more fervently. Let their wisdom teach you as much as you teach them.

● Hold a "stump the teacher" night during which youth write hard questions about faith and God and life. Your goal is not to be stumped as much as to give youth a comfortable way to lay their questions on the table.

Once the questions are out, show how each one stumps you at least somewhat. Affirm that according to Matthew 7:7-8, God welcomes our search for answers. Explain also that most Christians still struggle with unanswered questions, and we can help each other on the road.

Invite each young person to pick a stumping question, to tell one reason it bothers him or her, and to name one possible hint for the answer.

● To learn what's going well and what could be strengthened in your group, regularly invite youth to privately evaluate what's happening in your youth group. The churched youth may be some of your wisest evaluators. Though you won't distinguish them in the question asking, you may want to privately thank some for their insights. Ask one question at a time. Here are some questions to ask:

■ What are the strongest and weakest factors in our youth group right now?

■ On a scale of one to ten, how closely do our Bible studies match your life? Why did you give this ranking?

■ What one topic or question would you like us to address?

■ How can we as a group be truer to God in the way we treat each other?

● Each week, teach a new welcoming strategy to help youth reach out to visitors and to each other. Here are some examples:

■ "When a guest comes, you two open the seat between you. Then she'll be right in the middle of the conversation."

■ "Will you stand by the door and say 'hello' to every teenager who comes in?"

■ Deliberately say 'hello' and ask a question of six people each time you're here. Make certain you vary that six so you get to talk to everyone in the group regularly."

● Show youth how to visit a funeral home (Ecclesiastes 3:4). The first time most people visit a funeral home is when someone they care about has died. Then they don't know what to say or do to be genuinely helpful. They resort to clichés that hurt more than help. So show youth how to help grieving friends before death happens. Let them generate what to say and what not to say, what to do and what not to do, how to listen without interrupting, and how to remember the deceased person.

- Together generate a list of fifty ways to minister to someone in crisis. First list crises (death of a friend or family member, serious illness, car accident, move, crime, and so on). Then match to that list at least fifty ways to care. Put with each crisis the actions that would help that situation most. Be sure to include "Ask what they need and then do that." Here are some other ideas: get homework, take notes and photocopy them, report happenings at school, give a gift a day while in the hospital, write the crisis event on your calendar so you can ask about it later, go with your friend to the doctor, and so on.

- Churched youth are rightly bothered by fakes and hypocrites. So hold a truth emphasis during which you ask, "How can I be true to God and to people?" First challenge the group to list all the ways we lie to God, then all the ways we lie to people. Generate at least twenty of each. Finally counter those lies with ways to be super-truthful in word and action. During this process, youth may recognize and repair their own untruthful qualities, as well as learn how to deal with the untruthfulness of others.

- To tap teenagers' need for significance and deeper growth, create ministry teams of three to six youth, every person on a specific ministry team. Begin by listing ways youth want to make a difference. Then generate teams that make those differences. Youth might say they want a closer group, they want adults to like them, and they want to do missions at home in between mission trips. One team then becomes the Togetherness Team, one the Church Relations Team, and one the Missions Team. Invite each youth to volunteer for the teams they feel best suited for, taking into account their spiritual gifts. Suggest they write their choices on cards so they feel less pressure to join a team someone else joins. If any group members don't sign up or if all sign up for the same team, call youth one-on-one to talk about good matches for them. Meet with teams to devise strategies.

- Establish a new privilege for each grade in your group so each year isn't just the same as before. Let youth themselves help you choose these rites of passage. Perhaps seventh-graders get to enter the youth group; eighth-graders get to be big brothers and big sisters to the incoming seventh-graders, showing them the ropes and sitting with them at youth functions to make certain they feel a part of things; ninth-graders get to go on mission trips for the first time and get to write the welcome notes for anyone who visits during the week; tenth-graders get to serve on the planning team that chooses topics for study and growth; eleventh-graders get to help plan retreats and other big events, visiting sites and developing everything around a theme they help choose; and twelfth-graders get to serve as family group leaders (see next suggestions).

- Lead youth in older grades to deliberately minister to younger youth. Let this be a rite of passage for your youth: "When you get to be a senior, you will be a family group leader. You'll lead, along with another senior, a team of youth. You'll serve as a model to them for living that week's Bible passage, keep up with their joys and sorrows, and build togetherness in your family." Don't just say, "Lead!" Instead give seniors three specific directions weekly.

- Develop a six-year plan (or seven or two or four, depending on the years in your youth group) so that each age group studies a different set of topics. This provides less "we've done that before."

- Get together as youth workers to name six good qualities about every member of the group. Keep this totally positive so each leader can benefit from the good every other leader sees in each youth. Go in alphabetical order.

- See the potential gifts behind what appear to be weaknesses. A young person who initially appears to ask obnoxious questions may have the spiritual gift of prophecy and may be prodding the group toward greater spirituality. A teenager who bounces around the room may be able to channel his or her energy into a doodling sheet that pictures just what the Bible passage says. A youth who is super-quiet may possess spiritual discernment; you could invite the person's feedback privately. Be cautious not to call bad good, but do look for the strengths in every one of your teenagers. And say what you see.

- Courageously explore classic questions that Christians have struggled with for centuries. Begin by assuring youth that these have no easy answers and at best, you'll find hints to the answers. Rather than just pool ignorance, invite each young person to share a Bible verse and an idea they think might hint at the answer. Finally, ask for Bible promises that help youth keep on keeping on while waiting for answers. For example, to address the question of why bad things happen to good people, a young person might cite 1 Peter 4:12, 19 to give the truth that suffering comes to us all (verse 12) and that when we suffer, God's will is for us to go ahead and do good as an expression of our commitment to God (verse 19).

Here are some classic questions to explore:

- Why do bad things happen to good people?
- Why do good things happen to bad people?
- Why do mean people seem to get ahead even though crime never pays?
- Why doesn't God answer out loud?
- Why is temptation so very powerful—even when we know it will

hurt us, why do we do wrong?
- If God knew Adam and Eve would bring so much pain, why did he create them?
- Where did Cain's wife come from?
- Where did races come from?
- What happened to the dinosaurs?

● Train youth workers how to respond to hard questions. Assure them that they don't have to have all the answers because we know the Answer, God himself. Also, no Christian understands everything. Here are some tips:

- "I don't know, but let's find out together."
- "That's a good question; I'm glad you're asking it. Let me do a little research." (Then the adult youth worker can come to you or the pastor or another Christian they trust and you can research books and Scripture together.)
- "What do you see in the Bible that speaks to that?"
- "That's a question that has troubled Christians for centuries. What hint from the Bible would you add to solving this mystery?"
- "It's never bad to ask questions, because real faith will stand up under questioning. Questions show you take God seriously."
- "The only bad question is one you don't pursue to the answer."

● Urge youth workers, including yourself, to resist the temptation to push questions away with "We aren't meant to understand" or "You just have to believe." An unquestioned faith has little foundation. Remember that cults push "don't question" so they can brainwash. True faith needs no brainwashing or mind burying. Refusing to think things through can open one to abuse or misinformation.

● Enlist three different youth to lead brief praise and worship for a few minutes at every meeting. Keep a list so everyone is invited to participate. Downplay music and play up God so more than musicians will feel free to lead worship. For example, say, "We're going to ask each of you to work in a pair or trio to lead praise and worship at one meeting. You can invite the group to share prayer requests or you can lead choruses. What other ideas do you have for this time when we focus on God?"

● When you share prayer requests, have one young person call for requests, one write them down, and one pray. The more teenagers help each other pray, the more they'll recognize they're full-grown members of the body of Christ.

● Dare to study tough topics, even the ones that make you blush.

- When you feel like youth are getting away from God's view on something, ask, "How would God act in that setting (remember he lived here in the person of Jesus Christ)?" or "What words would God use?" This not only prompts youth to look at things through God's eyes, it helps them see that God cares about and understands the details of life.

- When studying temptation, ask youth to tell three pulls to do it and three ways to overcome each pull. Most of the time youth know something is wrong; they just don't know how to overcome the pull.

- Add a "Why?" whenever possible to get youth to voice the reason for God's rules. As they voice his reasons, they will better understand God's character and God's love for them. Then they will know better how to love and obey him.

- Attend a church business session with group members to watch how your church does things. Don't go when there's a big youth issue being voted on, but when youth are just observing. Evaluate afterward, insisting youth say three good things for every bad (this avoids a gripe session). Ask: "What one improvement do you want to work toward in our church? How will you personally work toward that?"

- Guide young people to list five things they appreciate about your pastor and other staff ministers. Write and deliver these as a demonstration of mutual encouragement.

- Give youth pipe cleaners (or foil) and have them shape them into representations of actions they could take to make church as comfortable for other people as it is for them. Stress the mutuality of this effort: As youth focus on other people's comfort, their own comfort will deepen. And as they notice what makes them comfortable, they'll find ways to help others be comfortable.

- Study 1 Corinthians 12 with approaches like this: What verse do you especially like in this chapter and why? How are you a cooperating body-of-Christ part? What spiritual gift do you see in each member of our group (focus on one member at a time)? What verse challenges you? Name one sentence or action that would help you meet the challenge.

- Study at least a portion of Group Publishing's *Training Youth for Dynamic Leadership*.

- Write a postcard to each of your youth at least once a month, praising a specific way he or she has imitated Jesus. Keep a list so you write all group members and you don't repeat an affirmation. This can be short; don't worry about making it fancy, but do worry about sending the same number of cards to everyone.

- Remember that even the most confident-looking youth struggles. Remember that even the most struggling youth has confidence. Give attention to both by communicating high expectations to each teenager in your group, while not setting up any of them to live a double life. Show them how to strive for goodness without feeling that perfection is the road to Christlikeness (Philippians 3:12).

- Believe that youth are more alike than they ever are different. Build bonds, not distinctions.

- When you distinguish youth, do so in ways that affirm them as body-of-Christ members, people who contribute uniquely to the group.

- Trust that each youth has unique gifts to contribute and no youth is more gifted than another. If you rank teenagers, they'll rank each other.